Bossed Up

Bossed Up

A Grown Woman's Guide to Getting Your Sh*t Together

Emilie Aries

PublicAffairs
New York

I'd like to dedicate this book to my mother and grandmothers, a fierce trio of women who showed me what it means to love and care for others and have the courage to love and care for myself.

PublicAffairs
Hachette Book Group
1290 Avenue of the Americas, New York, NY 10104
www.publicaffairsbooks.com
@Public_Affairs

Printed in the United States of America

First Edition: May 2019

Published by PublicAffairs, an imprint of Perseus Books, LLC, a subsidiary of Hachette Book Group, Inc. The PublicAffairs name and logo is a trademark of the Hachette Book Group.

The Hachette Speakers Bureau provides a wide range of authors for speaking events. To find out more, go to www.hachettespeakersbureau.com or call (866) 376-6591.

The publisher is not responsible for websites (or their content) that are not owned by the publisher.

Print book interior artwork by Ellie Nonemacher.

Library of Congress Cataloging-in-Publication Data
Names: Aries, Emilie, author.
Title: Bossed up: a grown woman's guide to getting your sh*t together / Emilie Aries.
Description: New York: PublicAffairs, [2019] | Includes bibliographical references.
Identifiers: LCCN 2018053496| ISBN 9781541724204 (hard cover: alk. paper) | ISBN 9781541724181 (ebook)
Subjects: LCSH: Women—Vocational guidance. | Women—Psychology. | Career development. | Success.
Classification: LCC HF5382.6 .A75 2019 | DDC 650.1082—dc23
LC record available at https://lccn.loc.gov/2018053496

ISBNs: 978-1-5417-2420-4 (hardcover); 978-1-5417-2418-1 (ebook)

LSC-C

10 9 8 7 6 5 4 3 2 1

Contents

Introduction

Confessions of a Recovering Hot Mess

Confession: I'm a recovering hot mess.

It really began in college, where I operated more like a hurricane than a human being—I tore through my academic career with a voracious appetite for achievement, unbridled ambition, and a complete disdain for rest. When I wasn't in class or writing papers, I was at volleyball practice, working on the student newspaper, or volunteering for political campaigns. Hurricane Emilie, coming through. It wasn't uncommon for me to actually say, "I'll sleep when I'm dead," about my frequent all-nighters, whether they were for work or fun.

This, I was sure, was what success felt like.

And my report card confirmed it. Like so many young women, I had become quite adept at figuring out what my professors were looking for, putting my nose to the grindstone, and delivering it.

Perfecting, performing, pleasing. These are the skills I refined in school, and these were the skills for which I was rewarded. From gold stars in kindergarten to my grade point average in college, I graduated feeling like I had it all figured out. Give me a syllabus for life, and I was certain I could succeed.

Unfortunately, that's not how life after college works. Imagine my surprise when "real" life actually began.

Like so many millennials, I had the audacity to graduate right into the Great Recession. As anyone whose early career included navigating a recession-riddled job market knows, I was told I'd be lucky to find any work at all.

So you can imagine how fortunate I felt after a few months of boredom at a lackluster (but paid!) political internship in Washington, DC, when I was given the opportunity to take a leadership position as one of fifty state directors of Organizing for America, formed by then–newly elected President Barack Obama. OFA was the first-of-its-kind continuation of a presidential campaign that would serve as a grassroots arm of the administration and work to help pass a variety of policy reforms during the president's tenure.

All that hustle had paid off, I thought.

I hit the ground running and built an organization from the ground up, eventually recruiting, training, and managing more than two hundred volunteers across the state of Rhode Island, who took charge of organizing their communities, hosting phone banks and voter drives, and pushing elected officials to pass the president's policy initiatives, including the health-care reform legislation that would later afford me the freedom to start my own business.

Fast-forward a few years. The way I was working, well . . . it wasn't working.

Being busy had long been a badge of honor I was proud to wear, but I'd finally arrived at the point of diminishing returns. I was reminded of that old economic principle when I finally realized that no matter how hard I worked or how many hours I put in, my to-do list was ever expanding. Chronic overwork left me depleted, exhausted, cynical, and on the brink of burning out.

I was in the office until 9 p.m. or later most nights and habitually worked right through my lunch breaks. I started my days by bolting upright in bed in a panic, my work phone and personal phone in hand before my feet hit the floor, and ended them at political events or networking happy hours (more often they were one and the same). I was in a frazzled frenzy of trying to prove myself worthy of the opportunity I'd been given.

Ironically, I was working myself to the bone even without the direct, in-person supervision of any fellow staff in the state. As a single-staff state director, I had a level of autonomy enviable for many of my fellow recent grads, which was great, except I didn't use that power to set myself up for long-term success. Instead, I ran myself ragged, while joking that I was fortunate to be my own boss at such a young age but that "I was a bitch to work for." Oof.

Contributing to my misery was the fact that I'd gone from being a college athlete to having no real fitness in my life at all—for nearly three years. I bristled at my annual checkup when my doctor asked what I was doing in terms of exercise and my answer was walking my dog sometimes.

Worse yet, I used to tell myself—at least during the most intense months of campaign season—I was "skinny" because I couldn't find time for lunch. I remember, sitting around a health-care policy-makers' table in 2012 joking with two lobbyists that, hey, at least we got some protein in our breakfast from the soy milk in our coffee. Hilarious.

During this time, my once-close friendships took a hit, too. I rarely put in the effort necessary to keep key friendships with my college besties and childhood friends alive. I genuinely didn't think it was a big deal that I felt isolated and alone most days, and told myself that I was making sacrifices for a job I loved.

All this was complicated by the fact that I felt stuck in a completely toxic relationship. When I stepped up into the state director role with OFA, I'd just moved in with my boyfriend of a year, a fellow politico ten years my senior, who I'd met on the campaign trail in college. He was elected to local office, a passionate advocate for working people working on behalf of many social justice issues I believed in. He was smart and hardworking, and he also happened to be an alcoholic. The former impressed me instantly. The latter took me quite a bit longer to pick up on, and, once I did, I had no idea how to handle it (somehow addiction wasn't a topic covered in all my years of formal education).

Everyone has their breaking point. Mine happened one day as I was driving through my alma mater's campus in the fall of 2012. My organizing work often brought me back to the charming East Side of Providence, at Brown, where I'd just spent four years studying political science, getting my education. I was stopped at a red light while racing between events, bone tired and slumped over my steering wheel. It had been a particularly crazy day, and I found myself wondering how the hell I'd gotten here. Just a few years ago I was one of those students on the other side of my windshield. I was someone who used to feel in control of life. This was decidedly *not* the life I'd imagined for myself, and, though I was proud of the work I was doing, I felt misaligned and out of sync.

I watched as college students saddled with heavy backpacks crossed Thayer Street in the crosswalk before me. Sure, they looked pretty beleaguered too, but they were heading home for Thanksgiving break. As they rolled their bags across the street to the airport shuttle, I desperately wished I could trade places with them. I thought, "I'll gladly tackle your finals if you figure out my life for me."

In that moment it dawned on me: I was waiting for an end of the semester that would never arrive. I wanted permission to head home for a week and put my feet up on Mom and Dad's couch. Those same skills that got me so far academically—perfecting, performing, and pleasing—had set me up for a spectacular burnout.

This was depressing, sure, but I also started to feel bad for feeling sad. I felt guilty for wanting more when so many others had less. I thought of all the privilege I had going for me, all the opportunities I'd been given. My problems paled in comparison to those of the people on whose behalf I was fighting each day. So what the hell was *my* problem?

I just needed to suck it up. Do my job. Push through. Keep my nose to the grindstone, and surely I'd be rewarded, right? That's what I'd always done before, but, this time, it wasn't working. I was working hard but didn't know what I was working toward. I wasn't sure what I wanted my life to look like, and I sure as hell didn't know how to go about advocating for it.

As I sat there at the crosswalk, tears of frustration started rolling down my cheeks. I was tired of being tired. I was sick of feeling like I was in the passenger seat of my life, just watching the world pass me by. I was done waiting for permission to start living a life that made me happy. It was time to stop looking for "the right answers" and start figuring out what felt right *for me.*

As this fire rose up in me, I also realized that if I want to be in this fight for the long haul—if I want a career with real and lasting impact—the way I was working was unsustainable. I felt like I was just barely making it through each week, hardly keeping my head above water. I was going to have to stop sprinting through life and start training for my career like a marathon. And no one else could—or would—steer my life for me.

Sitting there in the driver's seat, I straightened up. Dried my eyes. The light turned green. I drove off feeling an unfamiliar sense of presence behind the steering wheel. I no longer wanted to be that harried, self-deprecating Hurricane Emilie. A calm confidence started to wash over me, and the cityscape outside seemed to move by my window more slowly.

This was the beginning of a rocky two-year journey full of reading, reflection, research, and experimentation to figure out how to own my power and step up as the boss of my own life—without apology.

My story is hardly unique. Along the way, I learned that so many of us are suffering in silence, feeling like we're stuck playing a supporting role in our own life story. So many of us feel like life is happening *to* us instead of the other way around. Many of us feel like we have no choice, no power, and no options when it comes to how we steer our lives forward. Or perhaps we find ourselves achieving hollow success, still unsatisfied when we get what we thought we *should want* only to find out it's not all it was cracked up to be.

And when our personal lives get in the way of our professional ambitions, we feel guilty and worry whether the two should intersect at all (spoiler alert: they always do). Exhausted, we might find ourselves asking, When is it time to stop achieving just for the sake of achieving and start designing the life we would *love* to live for ourselves?

I witnessed so many of my friends struggle through those internal conflicts, but my fellow young women seemed hobbled by hesitation in a way my male peers just . . . weren't. As much as we may hate to admit it, there's a sort of appeal to being a hot mess. I caught myself being especially demure and self-deprecating around prospective romantic partners, downplaying my achievements and ambition and playing up my overwhelm. The flustered young lady is often depicted as cute, loveable, and attractive to a suitor waiting in the wings to play the role of Knight in Shining Armor. This is something that is deeply ingrained in our culture and took me years to unpack (and, yes, we'll be talking about it much more in the chapters ahead).

But if you're a flustered young guy? The attitude is, well, you should get your shit together, bro.

This double standard is constricting for all of us. Men should be able to feel lost and unsure without reproach. And women should be able to own our lives with unapologetic swagger without being seen as bossy or braggy.

But here's the truth: It's hard to get out of the habit of living the hot mess lifestyle. It's not easy to assert control in your life, get out of the cycle of burnout, and aim for a more sustainable success instead.

We have to put our own oxygen masks on first so we're better able to help others—and because we deserve some fucking oxygen, too!

The basic principles behind self-care shouldn't be radical, but they are—now more than ever. Investing in your personal sustainability is an especially subversive act for women, who have long been lauded as the martyrs of the family.

In a world that's always placing more demands on our time and attention, the pursuit of sustainable success is the fight to actually *use* the power previous generations of feminists secured for us.

**CARING FOR MYSELF
IS NOT SELF-INDULGENCE,
IT IS SELF-PRESERVATION,**
*and that is an act
of political warfare.*

AUDRE LORDE

From Rosie the Riveter to those shoulder-pad-wearing glass-ceiling shatterers of the 1980s, our foremothers paved the way to provide our generation with unprecedented choices. But that doesn't mean choosing how to design our lives is easy. We no longer have to follow the prescriptive path for success so narrowly defined by the man's world we lived in up until very recently. Now it's on us to mindfully design the lives and careers we would love—and do the work of advocating on our own behalf to make them a reality.

When I stopped my car at that crosswalk, my life was at a crossroads, too. I'd been waiting for permission to start reshaping my life and career, and for whatever reason seeing those students solidified my realization that it was time to make some big changes. I began asking for help (starting with my primary-care physician, who gave me tons of insight into what addiction really was and got me into the office of a very capable therapist). I began clarifying my vision for my life—and what aspects of that vision I wasn't willing to compromise on.

Eventually I summoned the courage to leave that relationship, which had become increasingly abusive. I spent nearly six months couch-surfing with friends while I worked to get out of the lease I had with my ex. In the meantime, I found an incredible new job at a political strategy firm focused on digital media that would take me back to DC, the city I'd always wanted to call home.

I racked up about $6,000 in breakup debt (which is a *very* real thing we should talk about more), but it was all worth it. I moved into a one-bedroom basement apartment with not much more than my dog, a coffee table, and a mattress on the floor. Despite being in a fragile state, I felt happier than I had in years. The feeling of the blank slate before me was thrilling. I was ready to rebuild my life, on my own terms.

As I started down the road to rebuilding the career and life *I* wanted, I heard from so many others who were navigating life's inevitable rocky transitions, too. It felt good to know I wasn't alone and that, in fact, so many of us women struggle to claim our power to design the life we want for ourselves from the get-go. All the reading, research, talking, and experimentation I did over the course of those tumultuous years led me to start Bossed Up, an organization that helps other women break the cycle of burnout and craft a happy, healthy, and sustainable career path on their own terms.

Now, almost six years later, hundreds of thousands of women across the world have attended our trainings in person, listened to my biweekly podcast, or accessed our free online resources to learn new ways to own their power and step up as the boss of their lives and careers. This book is an extension of that work, and I'm so thrilled to finally share it with you.

This book is for the recovering hot mess who, like me, finally reached a breaking point and is ready to step up as the boss of her life. This is for the wanderer who's feeling stuck and is looking to clarify her purpose and gain new tools for making it a reality. This is for the burned-out overachiever who's realized it's time to stop performing for everyone else and start designing a life that will keep her sustained and satisfied for the long haul. It's for the boss who's always one step ahead, looking to gain new strategies for next-level, long-term success. And, yes, this book is for anyone feeling isolated and alone while facing major life changes.

You are *not* alone. Although I believe in the power of taking personal responsibility for your choices, you don't get to a life you love any faster by going it alone. We all need a squad of support to get us through life's tribulations and triumphs without losing our sense of self. And there's no need to expend energy seeing each other as competition. Bossed up women lift as we climb, bringing those behind us up the ladder of success with us.

Getting bossed up is about owning your power, knowing your worth, and designing your career and life accordingly. In the pages ahead I'll walk through how to ditch the martyrdom mindset that holds so many women back, and I'll unpack the steps to cultivate a boss identity and see yourself as the leader you've been waiting for. I'll dive deep into three core skills needed to pursue sustainable success: honing your assertive communication, cultivating resilience, and managing multiple long-term goals. Finally, I'll get into building a community of courage to turn to when you're navigating big life transitions.

You'll hear more about my life and career along the way, too, but that's certainly not the focus of this story, because the concept of getting bossed up is so much bigger than my company and me. For starters, the term "bossed up" is from hip-hop, an art form I've loved since I got my hands on my first Tribe Called Quest CD in high school. As a white girl growing up in suburban Connecticut, I was lucky enough to be raised by a dad who considered it part of his parental duties to give me a musical education that included everything from Beethoven and the Beatles to the Wu Tang Clan and Beastie Boys (thanks, Dad!).

So when I started to take my power into my own hands, it's no surprise that hip-hop was there to encourage me each and every step of the way. After all, if anyone knows about rising up in the face of injustice and hardship, it's black America. I think that's part of the reason why hip-hop culture has gone so mainstream—it's telling the modern-day version of the American dream.

We all bring different privileges, challenges, and perspectives to the table, and I always strive to bring an intersectional approach to how I think about those differences. In each chapter ahead, you'll see a few spotlight stories that chronicle the real-life experiences of women in the Bossed Up community. I've had the honor of working directly with each of them at our flagship weekend-long training, Bossed Up Bootcamp, and have kept in touch over the years to watch them bounce back from burnout, rise in their careers, and assertively craft fulfilling lives, too.

These women come from all walks of life, different parts of the country, various industries, and diverse backgrounds. It's my hope that these real-life narratives help illustrate the principles covered in each chapter and inspire you to recognize that no matter where we come from, we all want the same thing: a happy, healthy, and sustainable life.

I hope you'll add your story to the chorus of women who've learned to own their voice and take charge of their lives, too. Join our free online accountability community now at www.bossedup .com and weigh in as you read this book to share what you're working toward and how you're stepping up as the boss of your life to make it happen. I can't wait to hear from you.

Alright, let's get bossin'!

Chapter 1

Combatting the Martyrdom Mindset

Mama the Martyr

When I was growing up, my mom was the one who spent the entire dinner party in the kitchen. She was the one who stayed up until the wee hours of the morning before our camping vacations so that we'd be fully packed *and* could come home to a clean house. She was the one putting in extra shifts before the holidays to make sure our eight-night Hanukkah haul and Christmas morning didn't disappoint.

My mom is also a caretaker by trade, a nurse working twelve-hour shifts at a hospital in Hartford, Connecticut, to this day. She helps bring new life into this world and cares for other mothers in their most vulnerable state. She and my dad had four children together over the span of twelve years, each of us more or less unplanned, as they readily admit with a laugh, especially considering my mom's area of expertise. They did their best to share childcare duties, and, truthfully, my father was quite an involved parent. He ran his law practice from home, and, while Mom was working, he was always shuttling little ones off to nursery school or us older kids to after-school activities. He prides himself on being the "Grill-master" of the household and makes a mean stir-fry, despite leaving the kitchen in utter disarray when he's done. I know my mom appreciated the effort, if not always the execution.

My mom used her personal and vacation days to help start a medical mission in one of the most remote regions of Haiti. About four times a year she and a group of doctors, residents, and fellow nurses transport everything needed for a fully equipped operating room to Dame Marie, a small seaside village on the westernmost tip of the island. There they spend a week at a time providing critical OB-GYN care for residents who otherwise wouldn't have access to it, and train local medical providers, too.

My mom was born in Barranquilla, Colombia, and was raised in South America before moving to the United States at the age of thirteen. Fluent in Spanish, she was the perfect person to take the lead on these medical mission trips—first organized in Costa Rica, the Dominican Republic, and elsewhere in the Spanish-speaking world before setting up a permanent connection with community leaders in Haiti. My mom spearheaded acquiring all the necessary materials, managing volunteers, and dealing with the hospital administration. When she was recognized for her ten years of mission service, the Catholic hospital where she works named her a "Healthcare Hero," and the headline in our local newspaper covering the award ceremony read, "Teaching, Caring for Others Is Aries' Lifelong Mission." I'm so incredibly proud and in awe of her.

But, like most caretakers in our money- and power-obsessed culture, rewards and recognition are few and far between. And although I know my mother gets satisfaction out of her work, I worry about the toll it's taken on her along the way. When someone is so anchored in how she cares *for others,* she seems to leave little room for taking care of herself.

Of all the years I've witnessed her in action, I've never seen her put herself first—not once. Exhaustion remains the most common state you'll find her in, to the point where she actually looks forward to her mission trips to Haiti to get away from the myriads of responsibilities that await her at home. For working-class moms like mine (who have never had the luxury of opting out of the workforce) and for any women who pursue an ambitious career path, this feeling of overwhelm is a familiar one.

Although some progress has certainly been made, full-time working mothers still shoulder twice the childcare and household duties of full-time working fathers.[1] And this doesn't just apply to mothers, either. Women from all walks of life report higher levels of **role overload,** that guilt-inducing state of wearing so many hats in relation to so many people. Far too often the "emotional labor" of managing the household or office, including all the communicating and coordinating that go into daily life, falls invisibly on women's shoulders. These roles we play and the responsibilities that come with them are in constant competition for our limited time and resources. We want to be a good employee but also be there for our friends. We want to be a good city councilwoman but also a caring daughter. We want to be a good boss and also be present in our children's lives. For all of us, "the second shift" of labor awaiting us at home is alive and well as much as it was when Arlie Hochschild coined the term in the 1980s.

When we try to be everything to everyone, we set ourselves up to feel inadequate. We widen the gap between who we are and who we feel we *should* be—and that dissonance is the birthplace of guilt and shame. I witnessed my mom struggle with this my entire life, and I found myself following in her footsteps as I began to define myself as a young adult.

I felt like I had to deliver 100 percent for my boss, my boyfriend, and my family. When my ex and I adopted a puppy, I became the primary caretaker pretty instantly. He always put his work first, and I felt like if I didn't take care of our pup during the busy workweek, no one would. The idea of going to the gym when there was a steady stream of mission-critical work to be done felt self-indulgent, or worse—like that whole concept of self-care was for people with less demanding jobs. When we moved in together, I ended up doing the vast majority of grocery shopping, cooking, and cleaning in our little household. If I didn't do it, I mused, it wouldn't be done right. On the weekends, many of my campaign volunteers were hosting events and voter registration drives, and there was always some political event that needed staffing. I showed up because I didn't want to let them down, and deep down I believed they needed me. All these teeny-tiny choices added up, and soon I felt like I had no choice at all.

I fell right into the role overload trap that's set for all of us women, until I realized there's a vastly different way forward, one that requires hacking into our broken system of gender roles and overwork to carve out the kind of life and career I would love. In my own personal sphere, that meant getting clear on what I wanted for myself and assertively adding what mattered most to me to my daily priorities. I had to learn to guard my time, energy, and boundaries, and tolerate the discomfort that comes with sometimes disappointing others in pursuit of making *myself* proud.

It's Not You

At the risk of stating the obvious: this is not our fault.

We live in a burnout culture, where overwork and martyrdom are celebrated in countless ways that especially hold women back. We're socialized our entire lives to believe that this kind of performance—an endless pursuit to care for others—is what makes a woman worthy. Women who are kind, caring, generous, and nurturing are aligned with traditional gender roles and are socially rewarded for it. The little girl who lends a helping hand in preschool is considered a "sweetheart," and as that little girl grows up and enters the workforce, she's expected to be a cooperative and helpful coworker, too.[2] As for women who don't fall in alignment with these traditional roles? They risk being seen as selfish, bossy, braggy, or—the catch-all term for a woman who doesn't act according to societal norms—a bitch.

But although society sure seems to *like* women who take care of everyone around them, we don't actually *value* caretaking much at all. The Census Bureau estimates that there are currently 44 million unpaid elder-care providers, most of whom are women, taking care of aging parents and loved ones in the United States today.[3] None of them receive a stipend or tax break, and many of those caretakers have absolutely no workplace protections or family leave. Their work is almost completely invisible, unaccounted for, and uncompensated in our global economy.

The arrival of a new child isn't handled much better in the United States, either. We're the only industrialized nation in the world that doesn't offer parental leave for all workers. In fact, barely more than 10 percent of Americans are lucky enough to have any paid family leave at all.[4] We certainly made progress with the Family and Medical Leave Act, passed in 1993, by mandating some unpaid parental leave and job protection for qualified workers who had to tend to qualified family obligations, but even that extremely limited support applies to only 40 percent of the workforce. And who the hell can afford to take *unpaid* leave upon the arrival of a child? Not most of us.

Finally, when you look at the caring *economy*, it's hard to say that our nation cares much about professional caretakers, either. The people who are changing our aging family members' bedpans, watching our babies while we work, and educating our future generations during the most developmentally critical preschool years are among some of the lowest-paid workers in our entire economy. And, in an ironic twist, these workers often don't have access to family leave for themselves, either.

So where does that leave us? Well, for me at twenty-four, I felt torn between two hopeless alternatives: focusing singularly on pursuing a high-octane, well-paid career that would make me feel like I would be selfishly dropping the ball on my home life or the thankless, exhausting alternative of only and always caring for everyone else around me. When we women try to live up to these impossible, paradoxical expectations, it's no wonder we end up feeling taken for granted, undervalued, and resentful. In those early years in my career, by not choosing at all, I essentially chose *both* of those bad options. I was pursuing an ambitious career path while trying to be everything to everyone at the same time. So of course I wound up burned-out. I felt like I was stuck tap dancing on a tightrope—performing an impossible balancing act that everyone was bound to critique anyway.

I see so many of us—my mom and me included—internalize all these judgments and adopt what I call a **martyrdom mindset,** a psychological one-two punch that combines all the baggage of female gender roles with the Protestant work ethic that's woven into the fabric of our nation. That work ethic—for better or worse—connects people's *worth* with their *work.* The Puritans who landed on Plymouth Rock back in the day believed that a good person is a productive person. Leisure time was seen as evil—literally! Ever heard the saying, "Idle hands are the devil's workshop?" Guess where that saying originated.

Today's martyrdom mindset, in its simplest form, is the underlying belief that success requires suffering. It requires sacrificing yourself for others. Inversely, it's the belief that success achieved without suffering is somehow cheap or shallow. Think about it—do you fundamentally believe that to be true?

This philosophy has a viral life online, where career inspiration includes many a mantra like "Hustle hard," "Can't stop, won't stop," and "Rise and grind." Much of this culture is embraced by women and men alike, but it all manifests quite differently in a world that still holds women up to double standards that men just don't have to deal with.

Hell yeah, be a #girlboss, but like, do you have to be so pushy about it? Rise and grind, for sure, but can you make the kids breakfast first? Hustle hard all day every day to launch your own start-up, but also don't forget that your aging parents are relying on you to check in on them. In a world where women don't have equal pay for equal work, much less equal leisure time to devote to taking care of themselves or furthering their goals, gender confounds the Protestant work ethic to leave women suffering far more for far less.

Now, the difference between working hard and *suffering* to get what you want might simply be a matter of intensity, but a good differentiator to keep in mind is that the martyrdom mindset makes us fundamentally uncomfortable with leisure time. It can manifest an almost compulsive need to fill our plates until they're overflowing with obligations and duties—whether it's the unpaid labor in our family lives or multiple side hustles. When you're living with the martyrdom mindset, being busy is a badge of honor. Self-sacrifice is something you're proud of; it's what pushes your personal care to the bottom of your to-do list every single day. It's what makes you justify being chronically exhausted. It's what causes us to stop taking care of our own body and mind. Over the long term, we feel resentful. We want to be lauded for our sacrifices, and we expect others to sacrifice in the same way. If that doesn't happen, we feel unappreciated.

The most troubling aspect of the martyrdom mindset is that it's not even effective. A growing body of research shows that happier, healthier people are more productive, focused, and harder working.[5] Taking care of your basic needs has been shown to improve decision making, increase creativity, and help with problem solving and efficiency. As it turns out, there's truth to the old saying "You can't pour from an empty cup." Basic self-care isn't just the *moral* approach, it's the more *strategic* approach. It leaves you in a stronger position to do better work, help more people, and have a bigger impact.

Furthermore, what kind of model does the martyrdom mindset establish for your team at work or your family at home? Parenting experts tell us time and again that children don't subscribe to the "do as I say, not as I do" practice that we all wish they would.

They're watching. They're mirroring. They're learning how to lead their lives based on how you're leading yours.

That became abundantly clear when this doozy of a question was lobbed at me as I was starting to come to terms with my burnout:

"How long are you going to live your mother's life, Emilie?"

I was in my therapist's office—a tiny space on the East Side of Providence I'd been going to for about two months after finding myself at my absolute lowest. I was there at the urging of my concerned primary-care physician and was sure it'd prove to be a waste of my time and (very scarce) finances.

I was there to figure out how to get my addict boyfriend the help *he* needed, or so I thought. I didn't need help. He needed the help. He needed to understand all the ways I'd been sacrificing for him over the years, all the ways I felt responsible for saving his life, even when he didn't seem to want me to.

What a recipe for misery.

"How long are you going to live your mother's life, Emilie?"

The question hit me hard. This horrible, piercing, insulting question. I love my mom and immediately felt the need to defend her. She had the right to live the way she wanted! She made her own choices as a grown woman! And, hell, I'm grateful for the many sacrifices she made for me. She put aside her happiness, her leisure, her comfort, and her rest for my siblings and me.

But behind all that defensiveness was an admission: I wish she hadn't. I wish we didn't worry about her health, her exhaustion, and her stress levels. I wish she enjoyed herself more, both for her sake and for all of ours. It was in that moment that I realized I didn't want that to be the path I follow.

"Not anymore," I replied.

That was step one, admitting that I wanted something different. The next step was acknowledging that this was not a *rejection* of my mom or even a judgment of her choices, I was simply freeing myself to iterate, adapt, and adjust. I was giving myself permission to get out of the martyr paradigm and chart a new course.

Once we acknowledge that we're still carrying around the psychological baggage of the Protestant work ethic along with the remnants of prescriptive gender roles that were expected of our grandmothers and mothers, we can begin to lay those burdens down. They're not ours to carry. They read like dated scripts handed down from generation to generation, and they're long overdue for a rewrite. Each time my mother sacrificed her own well-being to be of service to others, despite her pure intentions, she was setting the example for me to do the same when my time came.

The truth is, we can edit that script as we see fit to better align with our own wants, needs, and expectations. Choosing to live differently is not a rejection, it's an evolution.

And in today's world, where it feels like we're witnessing an anti-woman renaissance and a long-overdue reckoning all at once, daring to care for yourself is a radical act. While a self-proclaimed pussy-grabbing president inhabits the same moment as the powerful #MeToo movement, staying vigilant about advocating for your basic rights is essential. We're living through a time of tectonic shifts in gender roles, where debates over safe spaces and civil rights are more omnipresent than ever.

It's up to you to internalize these macro shifts on a more personal level. It's time to forge a new path forward—your own path.

Our Choices ⟷ Our Culture

Mindfully deciding how to lead your own life and choose your own career path has broad implications. Our personal choices both shape our collective culture and are constrained by it.

For example, it's no wonder so many of us struggle with the martyrdom mindset and find ourselves stuck in this cycle of overwhelm—we're simply trying to *make it work* in a culture where burnout is the norm. Although worker productivity has risen over the past fifteen years, most Americans' wages have remained more or less stagnant, leaving millions feeling financially vulnerable even as hiring rates rise.[6] For those of us fortunate enough to be fully employed, the boundaries between work and the rest of our lives have been blurred beyond recognition. The relatively new *possibility* of being "always on"—work email on our personal phones, late-night texts from bosses, leaving the office and booting up the laptop as soon as we get home—has led many workplaces to *expect* it, which may be part of the reason Americans work more late nights and weekends than workers in any other nation.[7]

Stress levels have increased 18 percent for women over the past thirty years and even more for men, who continue to spend even more hours at the office per week than women. Americans report working longer days and retire later than workers anywhere else in the industrialized world. The US Travel Association was alarmed to learn that four in ten Americans leave vacation time on the table each year, citing a lack of time or money to get away, belying a deeper fear, I suspect, of being seen as less than fully committed to our work.[8] We actually *want* to be seen as the office martyr in a culture that applauds such devotion.

But when we make choices like that—keeping our nose to the grindstone instead of taking the vacation time we're entitled to, or spending our nights and weekends behind the glow of our laptop screens instead of spending quality time with friends and family, we collectively contribute to that new normal. When we make day-to-day choices with a martyrdom mindset that puts everyone and everything else before our own personal sustainability, we collectively construct our burnout culture. It becomes a self-perpetuating toxic cycle of churn and burn.

There's a bit of a chicken-or-egg debate raging about how exactly we arrived at this toxic workplace culture. Did our over-work culture come first? Or did our personal choices shape our culture? Some feminists argue that women's overwhelm is mostly due to our broken government's deteriorating social safety net and a broad burnout culture at work.[9] Others encourage women to just "lean in" more and combat our own internal barriers.[10]

I'm tired of being told it's one or the other. It's not a binary choice. We could all benefit from big changes on the systemic level through Congress and among the leadership ranks of organizations and businesses, *and* we can make small changes right now that start with us.

President Obama struck this balance perfectly when I saw him speak at the first-ever United State of Women Summit held in Washington in 2016, comments he later expanded upon in *Glamour* magazine:

> There's still a lot of work we need to do to improve the prospects
> of women and girls here and around the world. And while I'll
> keep working on good policies—from equal pay for equal work

THE MOST IMPORTANT CHANGE
MAY BE THE TOUGHEST OF ALL —
and that's changing
ourselves.

BARACK OBAMA

to protecting reproductive rights—there are some changes that have nothing to do with passing new laws.

In fact, the most important change may be the toughest of all—and that's changing ourselves.[11]

I believe in playing the cards we've been dealt, while changing the game. We can take the reins in our career and life right now to ensure we're living up to our own deeply held values *while* we lobby for change on a systemic level, too. We can advocate for what we need to be successful in our own careers *while* pushing for the social safety nets that would level the playing field for all Americans to do so, too.

Bottom line: I'm impatient. It's a trait that has served me well and has proven to be one of my biggest weaknesses. I quit my job (perhaps prematurely) to start Bossed Up because I wanted to get to work on these issues and didn't want to wait around for someone else to start the kind of organization I was looking for. I'm impatient with Congress. As someone who started her career lobbying elected officials to get things done, I became all too familiar with the glacial pace of policy change, even when working under President Obama, who I believe will go down in history as one of our most productive presidents of all time.

So my focus is on how *you,* starting right this very moment, can take the reins in your own life, despite the unjust stage upon which this is all playing out. Acknowledging that our culture can constrain our options, I'm focused on how *you* can make mindful—maybe even radical—choices about how you live and work that start to change our burnout work culture from the inside out.

And if there's ever been a time to focus on sustaining the change we want to see in our lifetimes, this is it. With the renewed

I BELIEVE IN PLAYING THE
CARDS WE'VE BEEN DEALT,
while changing the game.

EMILIE ARIES

activism and engagement we saw with the Women's March in 2017, which became the largest global protest in history, we know women are rightfully outraged about a culture that doesn't seem to validate our humanity. As we figure out how to harness our power and grow this movement *collectively,* we have to make sure we're sustaining ourselves *personally.*

In fact, I argue that all of us—each and every person looking to grow her power and advance her personal and professional life through reading this book—will be in a better position to advocate for the sweeping reform we all need, from a place of personal sustainability. Grow your power, and you'll be better able to grow the power of others. Lift as you climb. It's what bossed up women do. And, truly, it's what this entire book is designed to help you do, starting right now.

SPOTLIGHT

"I didn't think I could make more and contribute to the greater good."

Emma is a proud graduate of a liberal arts college, where she studied sociology. "There were a lot of women, people of color, and LGBTQ folks in my program," said Emma. "I felt like we were encouraged to enter more of a 'soft' major like sociology once it was clear that we cared about people and social justice." She never considered any other course of study, even when her parents asked what kind of job prospects might come with a sociology degree.

Upon graduation, she and most of her peers happily entered the nonprofit sector. Emma served as a nonprofit program manager for a mentorship organization in DC helping students get into college. She loved her work and had a lot of ambition and drive but was already starting to feel the pinch of a not-so-hot salary coupled with living in a not-so-cheap city. After attending Bossed Up Bootcamp, Emma successfully negotiated two raises and promotions in the following two years, and before she knew it she was the only young professional—and the only woman, for that matter—serving in a senior leadership role.

She loved being able to serve others through her work and was excited to bring her analytical thinking skills to help the organization operate more efficiently, maximize its funding, and use data analytics to make more strategic decisions.

But, after two and a half years, Emma started to feel like she was plateauing and wasn't being fully compensated for her contributions. It took her community, including a close mentor and a few friends, to take notice of her leadership and analytical skills and encourage her to consider a career in tech.

"Me? The nonprofiteer?!" Emma thought. "I hadn't even considered working for a *company* before. If I care about making a positive change, I figured I needed to stay in the nonprofit sector. Who cares if my salary is $30,000 less than my friends working at companies?"

Based on what she knew about the for-profit sector, Emma figured that if you're worried about the bottom line, you can't possibly have values or make strategic decisions based on anything beyond that. But, in connecting with the women she met through Bossed Up Bootcamp who came from other industries,

Emma's eyes were opened to the world of social-impact start-ups, companies that furthered a social good within a for-profit model. She was intrigued.

After years of paying rent in DC, meeting and marrying the love of her life, and rising in the ranks at her nonprofit, Emma was craving financial stability. She was committed to social justice and fighting for underserved communities, but the reality was, she wanted to pay down her student loans and start saving for a home, too.

"For a long time I felt like asking for more was selfish," Emma told me. "If I'm this middle-class white woman and I'm trying to make more money for myself, am I standing in the way of others?"

Despite Emma's trepidation, her positive impact was being noticed even beyond her organization and its community partners. She was tapped to give a talk at a major tech conference in San Francisco that brings together more than a hundred thousand data experts and tech professionals. Her growth in using tech for her nonprofit without an IT background and her record advising on data-driven decisions made her the perfect person to give a talk on becoming "An Accidental Admin," in which she shared how she was using technology for good.

Her talk led to contacts from a few interested consulting firms, and Emma quickly realized that her ability to communicate and think about the interconnectedness of people, culture, and society was, in fact, quite valuable in the tech labor market.

"Looking at strategy, focusing on communication, and building trust among teams were my strengths," Emma observed, "but up until then I didn't believe that I could pursue a job in tech *and* work for a company that aligned with my values."

That all changed when Emma found herself in conversation with a technology consulting firm that focused specifically on supporting nonprofits. Maybe she *could* do well for herself and continue to do good in the world. Maybe she *didn't* have to compromise on what she cared about in order to care more for herself, too.

"I had to get out of this mindset that there's only one way to do meaningful work and that it somehow required sacrificing my well-being, my financial stability, and my own long-term goals," said Emma. "By getting past that guilt, I realized that I could have an even greater impact fighting for the causes I care about by helping more nonprofits be smarter with their data and do more with technology."

Emma made the leap into the role of project manager at a nonprofit technology consulting firm and found that not only is she making $10,000 more a year, but she also has more flexibility in her lifestyle and is feeling more confident and valued than ever before.

"I realized I could make this career shift without compromising my values *and* it would afford me the time to volunteer and contribute to the local initiatives I care deeply about without making it my 9-to-5," Emma reported. "Just because society tells women we need to be on the grind, caring for others 24/7 to succeed doesn't make it true. Because guess what? That's not what men are doing. And me being on the go, working away all the time won't change that."

Okay, Back to Basics

Despite all the systemic challenges that constrain our choices, the first step to combat the martyrdom mindset, is to go back to basics. Our basic human needs transcend race, class, age, and industry. Psychologist Abraham Maslow's famous hierarchy of needs chart is as relevant today as it was back in 1943 when he first published *A Theory of Human Motivation.*

Maslow argued that all healthy human beings have certain fundamental needs that must be fulfilled for them to operate at their highest order of being—to achieve their fullest potential. You can't operate at your best before covering the basics first. The very foundation of a high-functioning human being starts with things

like food, water, warmth, rest, security, and safety. It seems like these are things most of our colleagues have on lock, right?

You might be surprised. You don't have to be on the street for these fundamental needs to be tenuous in your life. A high-achieving media friend of mine passed out in an elevator in the NYC skyscraper where she was working, only to awake in the hospital with extreme dehydration. She'd been working around the clock for too many consecutive hours and hadn't stopped for water. Arianna Huffington shared how she hit such a point of extreme exhaustion and sleep deprivation that she collapsed in her office, breaking her cheekbone on her desk as she fell to the floor.

We sometimes wrongly assume that our colleagues—especially those white-collar workers who seem like they have it all together—have basic needs like security and safety all taken care of. Only once I started sharing with other women what I had gone through while living with my ex did I realize that so many high-achieving women find themselves in abusive relationships, too. Whether you're facing physical or psychological danger, it impacts your basic sense of safety. I didn't realize how exhausting it was to live that way until I was resettled in a new apartment of my own after my six months of tumultuous couch-surfing.

And that doesn't even begin to unpack the financial insecurity that keeps so many Americans up at night. In the latest federal report, four in ten Americans said they could not come up with the cash to cover an unanticipated $400 expense without selling something they own or borrowing it.[12] A quarter of Americans said they were not "living comfortably" or "doing okay," including more than a third of black and Hispanic adults.

When we talk about women and money in particular, the conversation invariably drifts to the gender wage gap, because even today the average American woman earns only eighty cents on the dollar compared to the average man, even when you control for factors like education, hours worked, and occupational segregation. For black, Latina, and Native American women, the numbers are even worse: sixty-three cents, fifty-four cents, and fifty-seven cents respectively.[13] But few people realize that the *wealth* gap—which is a far better indicator of financial safety—is even bigger.

The wealth gap compares familial finances more broadly: accounting for all assets (homes, retirement funds, vehicles, and cash, among others) minus all debts (loans, mortgages, credit card debt, etc.). Those are the resources you have to fall back on in an emergency, to retire on, or to finance your or your children's education. This gap paints a more accurate picture of who's feeling deep financial anxiety, and the numbers are abysmal—especially for women of color. The average single woman owns just thirty-two cents for every dollar owned by the average white man, and black and Latina women own *less than one penny!*

The reality is, many Americans—including those who identify as being "middle class"—continue to live deeply indebted, paycheck-to-paycheck, financially insecure lives. These chronic insecurities and anxieties can add up and chip away at your psychological foundation.

So the very first step to getting Bossed Up is ensuring that you're not going to burn out. How can you assess your basic needs, starting right now? How are you measuring up when it comes to caring for yourself through basic nutrition, regular rest, and a sense of emotional, physical, and financial security? No one can build an empire on a crumbling foundation.

Here's a simple and quick exercise to use for self-assessing your own basic needs:

Try It!

In the wheel below, you'll see six lines representing some of the foundational basic needs in your life. A dot on the perimeter of the circle means you're feeling 100 percent fulfilled and satisfied and that need is being fully met. A dot in the center means that need isn't currently being met at all.

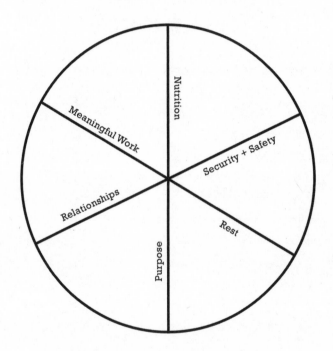

Place a dot on each line based on how you're feeling about that particular basic need right now, and then draw a line connecting them. Look out for valleys and peaks as feedback on where to refocus your attention and take even more care of yourself moving forward.

In the section ahead, we'll walk through how to prevent burnout from becoming your norm, beyond prioritizing your basic needs. I'll cover in detail the four main causes of burnout so you can prevent it from happening to you or begin to bounce back right away.

SPOTLIGHT

"At one point I was working five part-time jobs."

Lauren had always been told that education is the key to success. She grew up in a small town in Wisconsin, and when her parents divorced when she was just ten, times were tough. Her stay-at-home mom became the primary caregiver while putting herself through nursing school in order to reenter the workforce. Child support payments barely covered what Lauren and her siblings needed to get by, but Lauren's mom reminded her: if you work hard, study, and seize every opportunity, you'll make your way in this world.

"My whole life, people were always telling me I was smart and had so much potential, and that I just needed to work hard and take advantage of every opportunity I was given," Lauren remembered.

She took that advice to heart and committed to being a good role model for her younger siblings. Lauren worked her tail off in high school and was so excited when she was accepted into a small liberal arts college in Minnesota.

With a combination of federal loans, a generous financial aid package, and some college savings her parents had squirreled away, Lauren arrived on campus knowing she wanted to make the most of every opportunity. She had a work-study food service job on campus that helped cover her costs of living, but she stayed focused on her schoolwork.

But things changed dramatically in her sophomore year. Tuition rates rose, her scholarship package shrunk, and the college fund from her parents was sapped. Neither of Lauren's parents was in a position to chip in, so Lauren took on another job at a pizza place in town in addition to her campus food service position. It wasn't enough. Lauren landed a paid internship with a national advocacy organization, found a regular babysitting gig caring for a professor's kids, and started giving campus tours for the Admissions Office. Before she fully realized what was happening, Lauren found herself juggling five part-time jobs on top of her full course load.

"I felt like I had to do more to live up to who everyone thought I was back home," Lauren told me. "I wanted to make my family proud and be a good role model. I wanted to be strong, no matter what it took."

But Lauren's academics were slipping. She was so preoccupied with *paying* for college, she felt like she didn't even know why she was there anymore. Exhausted, Lauren was burning out and getting cynical. "What was I killing myself for, anyway?" she thought.

Exhausted and drained, Lauren faced a scary flare-up of a chronic illness, an autoimmune disorder she had lived with her entire life. She found herself so constantly tired that even spending fourteen hours a day in bed didn't revive her. She lost her appetite, recalling a day when all she ate were mashed potatoes and a bag of chips.

Her roommate grew concerned and booked Lauren an appointment at the campus's free counseling office. Lauren agreed to show up and after speaking with a counselor was diagnosed with a depressive disorder. That was enough for her to realize something needed to change.

"I didn't want to suffer to be in college just because I thought I was *supposed* to be in college," Lauren told me. "And anyway, with all the difficulty I was facing just to pay for it, I wasn't actually doing that well. My GPA took a nosedive."

At the close of the semester, Lauren took a job as a camp counselor at a summer camp for kids with special needs. Despite the intense mental, physical, and emotional demands of the job, it came as a huge relief compared to the full plate she was juggling back on campus.

As the summer was winding down, Lauren felt a sense of dread at the thought of returning to campus. What was once the promised land of limitless opportunity had become a panic-inducing nightmare. "It became abundantly clear that this path forward was not sustainable," said Lauren. "I gave myself permission, for the first time in my life, to take time off and figure out a more sustainable approach."

So at the end of that summer, without anything else lined up, Lauren made the scary decision to drop out of school and recalibrate. She spent the next two and a half years working, continuing on at the day camp and ultimately serving as a full-time nanny.

I met Lauren when she joined me at Bossed Up Bootcamp during this period of recovery and refocusing. She had just turned twenty-two and was ready to get back to pursuing her degree but, this time, on her own terms.

"I was stuck and needed a game plan for getting back to school, but in a new way," said Lauren. Her new path forward started with deep reflection. Lauren had to shake off the expectations she felt she had to live up to, the roles she felt everyone around her wanted her to play, and instead get clear on what mattered most to *her.*

That not only meant figuring out what she wanted to study, it also meant finding a way to make it financially feasible. Lauren ended up transferring to a more affordable state school that awarded her significant scholarships. She also successfully negotiated with her boss to keep her nanny job, but with clear boundaries that would preserve time for her studies.

"It felt so much better to approach my education with a focus on what *I* wanted to get out of it," said Lauren. "I was no longer just striving to perform for others. I knew what this degree was working toward, and that made a huge difference."

Taking time to reassess and get clear on her long-term goals became Lauren's guiding compass and a whole new practice she incorporated into her routine. "Now I'm reflecting much more often," she said. "I'm checking in and asking myself to consider if I'm taking on too much. I'm saying no to things that don't align directly with my priorities."

I reconnected with Lauren two years after she went back to school armed with this new approach and was thrilled to hear that just two weeks prior she had graduated with honors. The day after the graduation festivities were done, Lauren was overcome with emotion and found herself crying in disbelief. "I just couldn't believe I did it," she said. "After everything I'd gone through, even in those darkest moments when I didn't think I was capable of going on, to finally graduate left me amazed with myself."

Through it all, Lauren recognized that hard work alone sometimes isn't enough. Suffering for success is no way to strive for it at all. Sometimes, to be most strategic, you have to afford yourself the time and attention to step back, recalibrate, and find the right path forward *for you.*

"I learned I had to take care of myself first no matter what," Lauren told me. "I'm useless to other people if I don't."

Bounce Back from Burnout

When living with a martyrdom mindset for too long, you're likely to end up burning out, just like I did in my early career. Although you certainly *don't* need to hit rock bottom and burn out in order to take the reins of your career and life, far too many of us do. Whether you're reading this book to proactively gain control of your career or because you're feeling stuck, isolated, frustrated, and in need of support, understanding the basics of burnout will serve you well in your career. Whether it helps you keep burnout at bay, bounce back from it, or help a friend in need get through a tough transition, this is one of those situations where it's helpful to know thy enemy.

This is especially true because in our hyperconnected modern work culture, there's a lot of misinformation out there when it comes to burnout. Our work culture normalizes—and even glorifies—some of burnout's root causes, like a chronic lack of rest.

It's worth stating clearly that burnout is not synonymous with exhaustion. Burnout is a diagnosable mental health disorder, defined by the World Health Organization as **a chronic state of stress** and characterized by its three main symptoms:

1. Physical and emotional exhaustion
2. Cynicism and detachment
3. Feelings of ineffectiveness and a lack of accomplishment

The tragic thing about burnout is that it can strike the highest achievers among us. It's often the folks with the most passion, drive, and enthusiasm who can, over time, fall into habits that lead to chronic stress and thus cut their ambition short. Sprint too fast for too long without recovery time, and you won't go nearly as far over the long term.

But there is some good news. Unlike more serious mental health disorders like anxiety and depression, burnout can be somewhat easier to turn around. There are *many* everyday strategies and small steps you can take to stop and even reverse the harmful impacts of chronic stress on your brain.

To really bounce back from burnout, you have to first understand its root causes: a lack of rest, purpose, agency, and community. In other words, burnout happens when your basic needs go chronically unmet. We can certainly audit our basic needs via Maslow's hierarchy, but another helpful paradigm is looking at burnout triggers in these four key areas of your life:

1. Agency

You've got a micromanaging boss. Your kid's gymnastics schedule now dictates *your* schedule. You've got a chronic illness that limits your mobility. You feel trapped in your relationship.

We all know what it feels like when we lack agency. No matter what we do, control over our life is limited by some outside force, over which we have little say. No matter what we do, we can't directly impact our life outcomes. It might feel like you're riding in the passenger seat of your life, watching it all roll by outside your window, unable to grab the steering wheel and change your direction.

There are times in our lives when we consciously give up some of our agency in exchange for something else. We accept having to be in the office from nine to five each weekday in exchange for a steady paycheck, for instance. We take on the many responsibilities that come with having a child in order to bring a new human into the world. We get married for the stability (or at least tax benefits?) that the institution brings. We relinquish our own agency all the time in exchange for something else we value.

But when we continuously feel a lack of agency over our own lives—over the direction of our careers, over our everyday choices—we can set ourselves up to burn out.

2. Rest

You're getting six hours of sleep or less most nights. You work every weekend. You're glued to your work email every night. You're never fully off duty because you feel the need to be constantly available to your team. You can't remember the last time you did absolutely nothing for a day, much less took an actual vacation.

This one is more obvious, no? Consider how much time you build in for rest and renewal to your average day, week, month, and year. And when you *do* rest, are you actively or passively relaxing?

Our consumer culture likes to sell the idea of rest and relaxation in a very passive way: mani-pedis, sitting out by the pool, midday social media breaks. But there's plenty of science show-ing that active relaxation that gets your mind into a flow-like state can be even more restorative.[14] Things like playing an instrument, painting, taking a dance class, and other forms of exercise can be more rejuvenating than passively scrolling through your social me-dia feeds or consuming your favorite TV show on the couch.

When we lack passive or active rest and renewal in our lives, we increase our likelihood of burning out.

3. Purpose

You're making money but not making a difference in the world. You get frustrated when your organization wastes time on the small things and loses sight of the big picture. You no longer *believe* in what you're doing with your life.

My generation—millennials—seems to have turned pursu-ing their purpose into the new sign of "success," putting a whole new kind of pressure on themselves with an ever-elusive metric for making it in this world. Most Baby Boomers and Gen X-ers never had such expectations for their careers, which for many were sim-ply a way to *fund* their passions.

But whether we expect to derive a greater sense of purpose from whatever yields a paycheck in our life or from our pursuits outside of work, we humans seem to have an innate need to feel part of something greater than ourselves. Maybe it's leading a lo-cal Girl Scout troop. Perhaps it's rescuing orphaned squirrels. Or maybe it's scaling all the fourteeners in Colorado. Having a sense of purpose, an end you're striving toward, or something greater that you're pursuing can keep you engaged and ward off burnout, even when dealing with stress in other aspects of your life.

4. Community

After graduation, your besties dispersed across the country, and you find yourself struggling to make new friends where you are. You travel for work all the time and wind up alone in your hotel room most nights. You want to go see a movie but can't think of who you might ask to go with you. After your kids left the nest, it became less easy to find peers to share in a casual evening glass of wine.

At one point in time in my life I didn't think that being lonely was such a big deal. There's important work to be done in this world, after all. Being a hard worker requires sacrifice, doesn't it? Who has time to go out with a gaggle of girlfriends every night when you're trying to establish yourself? I thought being driven just didn't jive with having a jam-packed social calendar.

But I underestimated the importance of social connection and community. In fact, many public health professionals warn of an impending loneliness crisis in our world. Some studies have even shown that too much time spent alone can increase your mortality risk to the same degree that *smoking* does and be twice as harmful to your health as obesity.[15]

Despite the hyper-connected nature of our social lives online, there's just no substitute for the IRL relationships that leave you feeling a deep sense of being seen. And it's not just important to have family bonds—it's close friend bonds that help increase our longevity.[16] Friends help ward off stress, make us feel connected, and help us feel accepted just the way we are. Without such community, we become even more susceptible to the risks of burnout completely derailing our careers and lives.

—— • ——

Monitor these four foundational components of a sustainable life—agency, rest, purpose, and community—on the regular to see how you're measuring up. One easy way to do this is with my free downloadable worksheet, the Bossed Up LifeTracker, which you can download at bossedup.org/lifetracker now. It's a simple monthly goal-tracking worksheet that helps you stay out of the martyrdom mindset, keep burnout at bay, and stay focused on pro-actively crafting a happy, healthy, and sustainable career and life.

But keep in mind, we're not aiming for perfection here. At certain times in your life, different elements will feel more or less in check, but it's more *the practice* of monitoring them that matters. At the end of each month, before you look ahead to plan for what comes next, look back and reflect on how things went. Are you keeping those burnout triggers at bay? Are you pushing back on the martyrdom mindset and staying proactive about setting your own priorities? Regular, mindful reflection can help.

Aim to Sustain

We know that women face unique social pressures to care more for others than we care for ourselves, *and* we know that burnout work culture is prevalent in much of the US workforce in particular. So how can we push back on this status quo to craft a career and life that *actually* works? The key is ditching the martyrdom mindset and striving for **sustainable success** instead.

There's a better way of living and working, and it starts by investing in your personal sustainability as an investment in your career longevity. It reframes the concept of self-care as a time-wasting, selfish indulgence into the essential maintenance of your body, mind, and spirit to set you up to have the optimum impact in your lifetime. Not only is investing in your personal sustainability the *moral* thing to do (we women should be able to care for ourselves without guilt), but it's also the *strategic* thing to do (by caring more for ourselves, we're better able to care for others, too).

Striving for sustainable success requires putting yourself first, not *always*—but not *never*.

This is often a sticking point with moms I work with. I hear often from mothers that "you just can't understand what it's like before you have a child," and I completely agree. But what lesson are we teaching our children if mama is always the martyr?

My parents had two pairs of kids, as we like to say. My older brother, Alex, was born a year before I was. Then ten whole years later came Ethan and a year and a half later, Isabel. Alex shared his room with Ethan, eleven years his junior, and I shared my room with Isabel, with the same distance in age. When my mom was pregnant with Isabel, I remember turning to her, genuinely concerned because I had such an overwhelming, almost paralyzing amount of love for my baby brother, Ethan, I just didn't think there could possibly be room in my heart to love my soon-to-be sister as much.

"I just don't know if I have any love left in my heart," I told my mom, ten years old and teary-eyed.

She comforted me by letting me know that love didn't work that way. Love is not finite. Although she confessed that she, too, was often overwhelmed by the love she felt for all of her children, the heart finds a way to expand its capacity for love.

In the same way that love for your children is not finite, neither is love for yourself. Taking care of yourself isn't tantamount to taking *less* care of your loved ones or your friends or even your work. In fact, how mothers treat themselves sets an example for how the little ones around you will go on to treat *themselves*.

Actress Jada Pinkett-Smith shared in an interview how she—as an actor, mother, and wife—learned to get out of the martyrdom mindset and get on the path to sustainable success:

> I'll tell you something about being a mother and some of the messaging we get in this country about being a mother, that you have to completely sacrifice everything. You have to completely sacrifice every single thing. I think the re-messaging that we as mothers need to have and gravitate to is that you have to take care of yourself in order to have the alignment and the power to take care of others at the capacity that we do.[17]

Whether you have kids, aspire to have kids, have four-legged fur babies, or don't want any at all, how you treat yourself says something to the world about how it should treat women. There's that saying, "You condition others on how you will tolerate being treated." Not only is that true on a personal level, I believe it's true on a societal level as well. We are living through shifting times when it comes to gender politics in this nation. It's a time of reckoning, of clarifying what treatment women will and will not tolerate.

So if we as women want to change the way society has historically treated women, we need to start by setting a high bar for how we treat ourselves and what kind of treatment from others we are willing to accept. If you won't strive for sustainable success in your own right, consider the example you're setting for your children and your children's children, too. Because how you care for yourself today will be echoed for generations to come.

And if you *have* been falling into the trap of the martyrdom mindset thus far, know that it's never too late to adjust your approach. Throughout the course of writing this book, I've actually witnessed my mother start to let go of the martyrdom mindset in a major way. On the brink of being an empty nester (my youngest siblings are charting their course through early adulthood), my mom started shifting her focus in a way I haven't heard from her before. "I want to have more fun," she told me recently, "and I'm really starting to figure out what that looks like for me."

Earlier this year, my mom and I went on the trip of a lifetime together. For her sixtieth birthday, I arranged for us to return to her country of birth, Colombia, for an eight-day trip that included a few days in the capital city where my mother grew up, Bogotá, and a twenty-eight-mile trek through the Sierra Nevada mountain range to visit ancient ruins known as La Ciudad Perdida, the Lost City. It was the first time my mother had returned to Colombia since moving to the United States at the age of thirteen, and my first time ever seeing my mother's motherland.

Needless to say, taking that time away together was a powerful reminder of what's most important in life. As much as we both pride ourselves on the work we do, there is *so* much more to a rich and abundant life. Watching my mother embrace simple pleasures like our quest for the best *ajiaco* soup in Bogotá or losing ourselves in fireside stories from native Wiwa tribesmen in the rainforest was absolutely thrilling.

But what I appreciate most is watching my mother start to embrace the pursuit of sustainable success back home from vacation, too. Old habits don't go away overnight, but I'm hopeful. She's making the pursuit of a happy, healthy, and more sustainable life more of a priority, and that fills me with pride.

——•——

In the chapters ahead, I'll walk through the critical skills that you'll need to put this philosophy into practice in the modern workplace, to help you craft a happy, healthy, and sustainable career path, too. To me, that's what getting bossed up is all about. And it starts with stepping into the driver's seat of your life in a world that has historically preferred that women cruise along on the passenger's side.

Chapter 2

Cultivating Your Boss Identity

Our career paths begin like an open road. At first, the road seems so wide and full of possibility it can be overwhelming. I wavered between applying to the Peace Corps and pursuing a career in domestic politics just as Barack Obama took office. I felt nearly paralyzed with what felt like too many options to explore. But, eventually, I saw an exit I liked and took it.

After cruising off that exit ramp and into the excitement of the Obama administration, I began to settle into my new career trajectory. I got more comfortable in my role as a state director and grew my team of volunteers. As time went on, I was given even more responsibility. But I was so busy working my tail off, I'd never taken a step back to consider whether the direction I was heading in was what I wanted for the long term. To those of you who have been in the working world a while, I bet you can relate. Before you know it, you can find yourself stuck, feeling like those intersections are becoming fewer and farther between. At every turn, we make choices that can direct us a little farther away from that wide-open road—or so it seems.

But that wide-open road hasn't gone anywhere. All those possibilities? They're still there. As are the other exit signs that we passed up on or never got to earlier on in our careers. So if and when you find yourself cruising along down a particular career path but no longer enjoy the scenery like you used to, I dare you to look for that wide-open road in your rearview mirror.

Can we throw our careers in reverse and go back the same way we came? Nope. But just because the world defines you as a certain kind of professional, that doesn't mean you can't begin to imagine a different way. It all starts with expanding your boss identity.

Identity Work

Identity work is hard, but it's something you've already practiced a lot. You just have to look back at your childhood and early adulthood. Back then, we changed our identity all the time. One day we were a baby in diapers and the next we were *a big girl,* and *big girls* act differently. One day we started going to school—with a big-girl backpack and everything!—and had a whole new level of independence and abilities. Remember when you turned sixteen years old? Sweet sixteen! Perhaps you woke up on your birthday feeling just a tad different, older, wiser. And how about being dropped off at college? I distinctly remember the feeling of newfound adulthood and independence setting in as my family drove away after moving me in. I had a newfound ownership over my life—what was I going to do with it?!

At each of these milestones, we began to see ourselves and our capabilities differently, and our identities change rapidly. Although psychologists agree that our core personality traits (our likes and dislikes) are more or less set in childhood, the way we internally *see ourselves* is still in flux. Perhaps in school you tried on a few different identities that we've come to know through oversimplified high school dramas: the jock, the smarty-pants, the sweetheart. If you're like me, you had a bohemian phase and a party girl phase thrown into the mix.

The way in which we see ourselves dictates the ways we behave. When we know who we are, our actions stem from considering what *a person like that* would do.

But, as adults, the natural benchmarks that set our identities in motion become fewer and farther between. Perhaps we get promoted, setting in motion a whole set of shifts in how we think of ourselves in relation to others. We might even get engaged or married, spurring a new iteration of who we see ourselves to be in partnership with another. Maybe we become parents, making what is arguably the most seismic of all identity shifts that a person can experience. But, most often, if we don't take concrete actions to actively shape our identities, our environment—however mired in burnout culture it may be—will shape them by default.

If you have a micromanaging boss who doesn't trust you to handle basic tasks, for instance, you might slowly begin to question your judgment and see yourself as less capable, too. If you're with a significant other who is controlling, who belittles you or tells you—verbally or otherwise—that you're not worthy of his or her time and affection, you might start to believe it. If you constantly tell a self-deprecating joke about how lazy you are, it may become a self-fulfilling reality.

Protecting your identity from constant degradation can be especially exhausting for people of color. The term "microaggression" was coined by psychiatrist and Harvard University professor

Chester M. Pierce in 1970, referring to "brief and commonplace daily verbal, behavioral, or environmental indignities, whether intentional or unintentional, that communicate hostile, derogatory, or negative racial slights and insults toward people of color." These microaggressions chip away at your very sense of self.

Microaggressions against women are rampant in the workplace, too, and their impact is magnified for women of color, who experience the overlap of everyday sexism and racism. Simply retaining a strong sense of identity as the boss of your own life is a radical act in a world so often hostile to marginalized people.

The key to retaining a sense of ownership over your life—and truly the first step to getting bossed up—is building a strong **boss identity.** It's all about *seeing yourself* as the boss of your own life. And, to be clear, when I say, "the boss," I'm not talking about some hierarchical management theory. This is about being the boss of you—owning your power, knowing your worth, and actively crafting your career and life accordingly.

Actively cultivating your boss identity is the opposite of getting bogged down in the martyrdom mindset. Instead of getting stuck in the socialized gender norms of pleasing, perfecting, and performing, cultivating your boss identity is a way of closing the gap between who you are and who you aspire to be. It results in a stronger sense of personal agency and ownership over your choices. Sounds pretty stellar, right?

Keep in mind, no one can hand you a boss identity. Like strengthening a muscle, it takes practice and repetition to develop over time. More than anything, it takes a willingness to try new things.

Beginning to see yourself differently starts with *acting* differently. Cultivating a boss identity is an iterative process, much like designing and launching a new product. First, you launch with a beta test. Then you see how people respond to it, and then you take that feedback into account to adjust in your next iteration.

Researchers described this process in the *Harvard Business Review* with a simple example: calling a meeting to address a workplace concern.[1] Taking the initiative to call a meeting with your colleagues is a total boss move. No one *tells you* to take responsibility in this way. Calling the meeting is your way of showing that you are *willing* to lead in addressing a concern you deem important and want other people on the team to buy in. Instead of staying frustrated and agitated that no one else is doing something about it, you decide to try something totally new: stepping up to address it yourself.

Calling the meeting is your beta launch of your boss identity. It's a new kind of behavior—one that shows autonomy, leadership, and courage. It's a *choice*—an *action*—not a personality trait.

So then what happens? Well, your colleagues can do one of two things: they can either show up and take the meeting seriously (thus reinforcing your boss identity), or they can blow the whole thing off and ask, "Who died and put you in charge?"

That's the "feedback" phase of the iterative process, and it can be a doozy. When you're taking identity-expanding actions, people are going to notice that you're acting differently than usual. And, with any kind of change (especially at work), you might be met with resistance, friction, and pushback. Negative feedback can threaten the very foundation of your identity—of who you think you are and what you believe you're capable of.

In other words, your boss identity is built through the choice to assert your power *and* solidified by how others react to your action. If building your boss identity were like building a sturdy wall, your actions are the bricks and others' reinforcing reactions are the cement holding them together. Making boss moves without others affirming you is not sufficient—you end up just stacking bricks and building a wall that could easily crumble.

But when you make a bold leadership move (like calling a meeting, speaking up to voice a concern, or taking responsibility to get a new initiative off the ground), your community can also *affirm* your expanding identity. As more colleagues and friends validate your authority, you gain a new sense of confidence to step outside of your comfort zone again. Remember, authority isn't derived from hierarchy. It's cultivated by taking risks and winning the respect of your coworkers.

As this happens, your boss identity grows stronger. What was once just a peripheral beta test, a trepidatious moment of "Can I really go for this? Can I own my power in this way?" becomes more central to your core sense of self. "Hell yeah I can do this, I'm a boss!" As your boss identity becomes more established, you become more confident continuing to exhibit leadership behaviors and taking on new challenges.

So how exactly do you go from feeling unsure, or stuck in that "perfect, perform, and please" trap, to stepping confidently into your boss identity? You need to find or create a safe identity workspace to experiment within first.

Space to Try It On

Seeing yourself as the boss of your life is a gradual process that requires the freedom to experiment. This is especially true if you're feeling helpless, powerless, stuck, or lost. Building up your sense of leadership is a process that requires *doing,* not just *thinking.* Mentally psyching yourself up or trying to boost your confidence through bravado alone won't work.

Here's what that iterative process might look like:

Step 1: Take Purposeful Action

Although it might feel like reaching beyond your comfort zone, this first step is all about asserting yourself—even if it's in a small way. It's about taking one step toward making things happen.

We'll talk more about honing your assertiveness in Chapter 4, but for now it's important to recognize that the first way to start seeing yourself differently is to act differently, even if it means taking a "fake it till you make it" approach.

The whole goal here is to start to bridge that gap between who you believe you are and who you want to be. Let's take an example from outside the workplace. Let's say you've always struggled with staying consistently motivated to be physically fit. Step one to changing your own self-perception? Take a walk around the block. Buy some new workout gear that'll actually motivate you to put it to good use. Sign up for a trial week at your local yoga studio.

Step 2: Gauge Reaction

This next part is out of your hands (so brace yourselves, my fellow control freaks!). It's all about seeing how those around you *react* to your action. Don't try to coerce a certain kind of response; instead, sit back and watch what happens—it might surprise you. When you share that you started a new fitness regimen, do your friends roll their eyes? Do they complain about you skipping out on happy hour? Or do they cheer you on? Commit to joining you—and actually show up?

When you take the initiative to plan a night out with your partner, is he or she on board and appreciative? Or reluctant and resentful? When you invite your pals over for a money-saving at-home workout instead of that thirty-dollar spin class, do they judge you or thank you? Does your boss appreciate you taking the initiative to call that team meeting? Or feel threatened by it?

Step 3: Internalize

Whether the reaction is positive or negative, we psychologically internalize the response and store it away in the recesses of our memory. Whether subconsciously or not so subconsciously, that experience gets tallied into the cost-benefit analysis for the next time we consider asserting ourselves. When you get positive reinforcement, it builds upon your sense of being a leader. If you don't, it can chip away at your confidence and your boss identity, and decrease the likelihood of ever asserting yourself like that again.

But even when things don't go your way and you don't get the response you hoped for, identifying *why* can inform how to proceed next. Was it you, *really?* Or was your partner just having a bad day? Perhaps your boss is just feeling threatened because of pressure from the boss upstairs. We're often quick to internalize our failures and credit our successes to outside factors like luck or chance. Don't let that be your default. When faced with failure after making a boss move, be sure to consider what external factors led to the negative outcome, so that you're not over-internalizing the factors that weren't in your control.

The reality is, your boss identity is bolstered by positive responses and threatened by negative ones. But keep in mind Hillary Clinton's advice on this part of the process:

> Take criticism seriously, but not personally. If there is truth or
> merit in the criticism, try to learn from it. Otherwise, let it roll
> right off you.[2]

At this point, the cycle repeats. It's as simple as that, boss. To change the way you see yourself and what you deem *possible* for yourself, you have to experiment with the actions you're taking first.

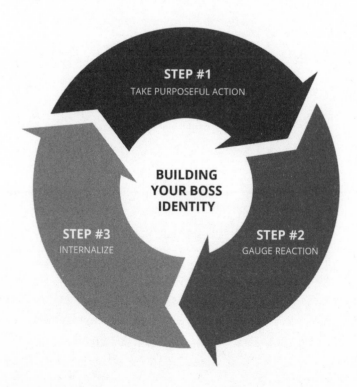

SPOTLIGHT

"I knew my team would have my back."

Jamie is a longtime member of the Bossed Up community, since she attended our very first Bossed Up Bootcamp back in 2013. After spending years serving on political campaigns as an organizer, constantly moving around the country, and never having a chance to pursue the sustainable life she wanted, Jamie set a very specific goal at the end of Bootcamp weekend: to land a stable job in health policy by February 2014.

She went on to do just that when she joined the team at Mission: Readiness, a nonprofit advocacy organization that lobbies on behalf of more than seven hundred retired admirals, generals, and top military leaders for public health policy solutions to prepare our youth to serve their nation in any way they choose. This is a significant challenge, because more than 70 percent of today's young adults cannot qualify for military service because they are not academically prepared, are too overweight, or have a record of crime or drug abuse.[3]

Jamie had been working at Mission: Readiness and moving up the ranks there for three years when the nonprofit faced significant financial challenges that resulted in a management shake-up.

One Friday, her boss's boss, the national director, announced that she would be stepping down and leaving the organization in the following months. The next Monday, as Jamie was preparing breakfast, she received a call from her boss, the deputy national director, who informed her that he had just been laid off and escorted out of the building. More layoffs were sure to follow, and he wanted to give her a courtesy call before she came into the office.

At this point, Jamie was in tears, uncertain of her future at the organization she loved. She felt abandoned, like the rug had been yanked out from under her, and it was all she could do to pull herself together and head into the office that morning, unsure of what awaited her.

But to her surprise, she found herself invited into senior leadership meetings, during which time the national director and other top leaders were discussing the path forward for the organization.

"I was just trying to keep it together," said Jamie, "when the outgoing national director said she was going to recommend *me* to take her place."

Later that day, Jamie found herself in the office of the president of the parent organization that directed Mission: Readiness. He offered her the job of acting national director, and Jamie was flattered but dumbfounded. She asked for a few days to consider the offer while she got her bearings and promptly called one of her trusted colleagues.

Should she? Could she? Jamie prided herself on her work ethic and performance, but she felt a deep sense of loyalty to her boss, who had seemed directly in line for the position but was just let go. Anyway, who makes a double leap up the leadership ladder like this anyway? She worried she wasn't qualified.

"Listen," Jamie's colleague on the other end of the phone said, "all we need right now is someone to right the ship. You can do this."

For Jamie, that reaction from a trusted team member went a long way in helping her see herself in a new light: as ready to seize the opportunity, despite the unknowns that lay ahead, and step two rungs up the organization's hierarchy.

"I knew there were larger organizational challenges for us to deal with," Jamie told me, recalling her decision-making moment, "but I had a really good team, many of whom I brought into the organization, and I trusted that they would have my back."

Jamie focused on just taking the next step forward, one at a time. Jamie spent the next few months transitioning into the role of national director as her predecessor phased out of the organization. She benefited from her hands-on coaching and mentorship while she got her senior leadership sea legs and stepped officially into the role in its full capacity a few months later. At first, she admits, she was intimidated.

"I was worried about how all the other stakeholders I'd be interfacing with would react," said Jamie. "I know I'm a young woman who looks *really* young, and there I was, representing retired admirals and generals, sitting at tables with health policy leaders who've been in this field for decades longer than I have."

But, with every leadership move she made, fortified by the positive, respectful reactions from her colleagues, her boss identity was solidifying, brick by brick. Although she couldn't match some of her stakeholders in terms of experience, Jamie realized over time that she brought other valuable skills to the table that had been lacking.

"I leaned on my tight relationships with our team members. People trusted me and wanted to help me make things happen,"

Jamie told me. "I was pleasantly surprised at how much I could get done by relying on my strong interpersonal skills."

In the role of national director, Jamie developed a democratic leadership style that was all about communicating openly and asking for staff members' input. As a result, her team members felt like they were being heard and had a real voice in the decision-making process. Their engagement once again reinforced Jamie's sense of leadership and helped her make better decisions.

"Throughout it all," said Jamie, "the fact that my team had my back is what carried my confidence through."

As we experience this iterative cycle of expanding our identity again and again over time, we must remain open to risk taking in order to reap the rewards. But you can see, then, why it might feel scary to initiate this process at a toxic workplace, in an unhealthy relationship, or in any kind of high-stakes social scenario. Being comfortable taking that initial action requires a safe space: an environment in which the potential risks are outweighed by the potential rewards.

The whole idea of schooling is to create a safe space for learning, experimentation, and, yes, sometimes failure. But. after we leave the confines of education behind, these kinds of spaces become more difficult to come by. That's a big reason behind why I started Bossed Up—to create safe identity workspaces in person (at our trainings) and online (through our community), where we can come together, try our boss identities on for size, and bear witness to one another's courage in action! We all need spaces like that—whether you join in on the ones we have at Bossed Up or not—and it's such an important part of the equation I devote an entire chapter to your community of courage later on in this book.

The hard thing about this kind of experimenting with leadership is that the risks can sometimes be prohibitive. Think about it—how much are you *really* willing to risk at work? It's hard to remain totally open to failure in the environment that provides your paycheck. Every time you make a boss move to expand your identity, you're taking a calculated risk, and that's not something I take for granted. Risk taking is easier, of course, when you have a whole lot of privilege already going for you—financially or otherwise. Of course trust fund kids are less worried about getting fired—they're not stressed about relying on public assistance to get them through the lean years as much as the single parent who's got mouths to feed. Similarly, the white dude at work can get loud and impassioned while disagreeing in that meeting, because he's less worried about being labeled as angry, emotional, and incompetent than, say, a black woman saying the exact same words, in the exact same way.[4]

Risk is always a factor to consider, but we cannot allow ourselves to get stuck in analysis paralysis forever. Taking purposeful action—no matter how small it might seem—is the first step to cultivating your boss identity. If you want to see yourself as the boss of your life, start by acting like it, one step at a time, even if the world doesn't welcome it.

And if your workplace is not the safe space you need to start putting that iterative identity-building process into play, find other opportunities to ask yourself, "Okay, in this scenario, what would a boss do?" Maybe that means stepping up to the front of the room in your next dance class, even though you're not 100 percent confident you know all the steps. Speak up at the next community meeting in your neighborhood. Spearhead a new book club or give yourself permission to start that side hustle you've been dreaming about. When we dare to flex our leadership muscles elsewhere in our lives, that confidence and courage directly translate to our workplace identities, too. To me, a boss is someone who owns her power, knows her worth, and actively crafts her career and life accordingly.

So when someone cuts in line at the concierge desk while you're checking into your hotel room, ask yourself, "What would a boss do?" That's exactly what happened to me in a hotel lobby, where I happened to be meeting all of Brad the boo's family for the first time together at a wedding.

As Brad and his family were chatting nearby in the hotel lobby nearby, I was checking into our room at the front desk. So I'm standing there, talking with a kind concierge, when a large gentleman, clearly frustrated, appears in my peripheral vision. He has a female companion in tow, her hands full with a half-dozen shopping bags. He sidles up beside me and tosses his room keys on the desk, toward the concierge.

"I don't know what to do," he bellows, "these still aren't working." He has momentarily disrupted the conversation I was having with the concierge.

With Brad's entire family looking on, I did a quick mental scan of the situation:

My options: Say something, or say nothing.

Risk level: Minimal. This dude has no power over me or my future. Lots of witnesses, very public location, no perceived danger.

So what would a boss do?

"Well," I said turning to him, "you can start by waiting in line, because I'm talking with this man right now."

Clearly, this gentleman did not see that coming, because he stood there in stunned silence, clearly disgruntled, but obliging. "I just . . ." he started, only to trail off. He sighed, and got in line behind me.

Meanwhile, Brad's entire family was looking on, equal parts surprised and entertained by my unabashedness. I'm pretty sure they fell in love with me right then and there. Brad, while not one bit surprised, was delighted.

Sometimes the words come to you just when you need them (if only I could be this quick on my feet all the time, right?). Sometimes we stumble our way through being assertive. But the important lesson here is that when the risks are too high at work, you can *always* find other opportunities to establish your leadership identity elsewhere in life. In fact, it's imperative that you do so you can feel like the boss of your life as much as the boss of your career.

I walked out of that situation feeling powerful and reminded of my own ability to stand up for myself—even in small ways—when I need to. That's leadership identity work right there, and it's a constant practice of flexing those muscles to maintain a strong sense of agency over your own life. When you dare to start by taking that first action, life no longer feels like it's happening *to* you. You no longer feel like a doormat, stuck in the cycle of perfecting, performing, and pleasing and living your life in the sole service of others.

It might sound trite, but standing up for yourself and advocating on your own behalf—even in seemingly inconsequential ways—is a radical act in a world that still isn't sure how it feels about powerful women.

The Call Is Coming from Inside the House

We'll start developing your leadership identity right here in just a few pages, but first I want to acknowledge some of the common challenges women face in getting started. I'm not mentioning these to dissuade you but rather to assure you that you're not alone when you run into roadblocks.

One of the most common pitfalls I see women run into (and part of why I was a self-identifying "hot mess" for so many years) is what researchers call the **impostor syndrome.** Have you ever felt like, at any given moment, someone is going to call you out for being a total and complete fraud who has no credentials whatsoever to be doing what you're doing? Well, unless you're living a legit con-artist *Catch Me If You Can*–style life, you probably experience this psychological phenomenon every now and then. The irony: the callout is coming from you, boo!

At its core, the impostor syndrome means you have trouble internalizing your own successes, even in the face of irrefutable evidence that you're doing something right. This tends to affect high-achieving people in particular, and studies show that it disproportionately affects minority groups. So if you're a woman— and yes, especially a woman of color—in a predominately pale and male executive suite, you become more susceptible to running into this utterly unhelpful mental loop.

Although you might have no trouble internalizing your failures ("Ah—I screwed that presentation up, I just can't speak in public!"), the same effect doesn't always take hold after you succeed ("Wow, leading that meeting went really well, today must be my lucky day!"). Instead of owning your success as much as you own your failure, you might chalk it up to good luck or any number of *external* factors. When we credit our failures but not our successes to our own actions, we're missing that critical third step in the iterative process of cultivating your boss identity: **internalizing.**

When I first stepped into the role of state director with Organizing for America, I told my friends that I had "talked my way" into the job, admitting that, deep down, I didn't feel worthy of it. I meant for it to come off as a coy joke, but it belied a deeper insecurity. As the youngest state director in the nation, I felt out of my league. I figured I got lucky. That sense of feeling like an impostor is part of what kept me stuck in the martyrdom mindset, feeling like I had to constantly prove myself worthy of the job I'd already landed! This anxiety continued well beyond the first few months on the job, and, despite my measurable successes, I was riddled with stress and self-doubt. I never felt that I was doing enough.

Was there an aspect of luck in getting hired to that position? Sure. But it also happened because I worked my ass off for it. I chased down the national field director at a political conference where he was speaking. This was a conference, mind you, that I volunteered to help set up and run check-in in exchange for the admission I couldn't afford. After his panel, I asked the field director some on-point questions about health reform and handed him my business card (which still listed me as a student based in Rhode Island). When he mentioned that he was looking to hire a Rhode Island state director soon, you can bet that comment didn't get by me. When he never emailed to follow up, I scoured my network endlessly until I found someone who had his email and was willing to share. I followed up relentlessly, finally landing an interview with the Northeast regional director (the woman who would eventually serve as my supervisor). And when that interview finally came around? I nailed it. So to say that I'd simply been "lucky" to have "talked my way" into the post was a gross understatement. I was prepared for good fortune to find me and to make the most of it when it did.

But I sure as hell didn't talk about it that way back then. I hadn't taken stock of what I'd done to land the job and instead accredited my success to luck. I wanted to be a humble, hardworking person, but I took those messages so far that I struggled to feel worthy of the opportunity. When you find yourself being your own harshest skeptic, cutting yourself down, and standing in the way of your own boss identity forming, it's time to beat back the impostor syndrome. Here are three steps to take to stop calling yourself out and get back to making those boss moves:

1. Phone a Friend

Loop in someone you trust and ask that person to walk through the scenario with you. We're often our worst critics, so get someone else's take on any situation in which you worry you're not measuring up, aren't qualified to even try, or otherwise feel like a total fraud. Make sure to ask men *and* women you trust for their take—and maybe don't go to your most anxious friend or family worrywart for this one.

2. Rewrite the Story

Identify the script of the mental loop you're stuck in, and write yourself some new lines. "I just talked my way into this job" was playing over and over again in my head for those critical early years of my career. I wish I'd sat down, acknowledged that anxiety-provoking mental loop for what it was, and written it down to get it on the page and out of my head. Once you identify the negative self-talk you're feeding yourself, you can write yourself a better story. I would have saved myself so much unnecessary pain and angst had I replaced that story with a new one—perhaps something like, "I worked hard to get here, and my boss placed her faith in me. If she believes I can do this job, I have to believe I can figure this out, too." The first story left me feeling anxious and inadequate, while the second would have helped me to proceed with calm confidence.

3. Ask "Why Not Me?"

Mindy Kaling, the creator and star of *The Mindy Project*, wrote a fabulous memoir that perfectly speaks to this angsty way of being. In it she asks a bold question I've found tremendously helpful for overcoming the impostor syndrome: Why *not* me?

So many bright, hardworking women trapped in this psychological ditch analyze all the ways they might be unprepared, worrying, "Why me? How am I possibly qualified to do this?" How about focusing a bit of that energy on what makes you uniquely prepared instead? "Why not me? I'm just as hardworking as everyone else here, and I bring unique perspectives with me that make me even more prepared to crush this!" Think about what makes you uniquely equipped to take the challenge on, and you'll put that impostor in your head to rest.

——•——

The impostor syndrome is one of those sneaky internal barriers that can hold smart, skilled, and oh-so-capable women back. Don't let it.

Another internal hurdle that makes cultivating a leadership identity especially challenging and exhausting for women is a phenomenon in the research known as **stereotype threat**. When women receive messages that tell us we're worse at any given skill than men, we expend energy worrying about proving that negative stereotype right and, in doing so, have fewer mental faculties available for the actual task at hand. Ironically, women reminded of negative stereotypes about women before performing a given task often *do* underperform as a result.

And sexist stereotypes are still out there. In recent years, a Google employee circulated what he called a "manifesto" in which he insinuated that women are biologically ill equipped for careers in STEM fields. When it comes to tired stereotypes like these, simply being reminded of your gender can have a negative impact. One study among high school students gave equal numbers of young men and women a math exam.[5] At the top of the exam, half of the students were asked to write down their gender. The control half of the study didn't have the question at the top of their page. In the control group, the young men and women scored nearly the same. When prompted to write down their gender, however, women performed worse than their male counterparts—*and* worse than the young women in the control group.

The problem is, negative gender stereotypes don't just apply to math exams. The modern workplace is a minefield of tasks associated with gender stereotypes. Being a leader, an effective negotiator, and a passionate advocate are still too often associated with masculinity, while being helpful, quietly supportive, caring, and kind are all associated with femininity.

Take this study as an example: A group of MBA students were paired up and asked to negotiate the purchase of a company.[6] Half of negotiating pairs were given information before the exercise that women are "often not effective negotiators because they are not assertive, rational, decisive, forceful, and unemotional." The other half were given neutral information. Those women in the stereotype threat group ended up confirming the stereotype, performing worse than the men, while women in the control group performed just as well as their male classmates.

Dealing with this kind of BS in the workplace was found to be "a primary cause of women's greater workplace stress." But fear not: researchers Andrea S. Kramer and Alton B. Harris found these effective, proven ways for dealing with this crap without losing your head:

> Dealing with stereotype threat effectively requires women to employ smarter strategies, such as imagining themselves as stereotypical men—tough, risk-taking, and competitive—for a few minutes before engaging in a task with potential stereotype threat; reminding themselves that the anxiety they may experience when performing a task with a negative gender stereotype has nothing to do with their actual ability and everything to do with stereotype threat; and avoiding viewing themselves through a gender lens ("I am the only woman in this meeting") instead of focusing on their achievements and abilities ("I am the only person in this meeting with an MBA").[7]

In other words, it's about adjusting your *identity.* Focus on your strengths and capabilities, remind yourself of all the purposeful actions you've already taken to get here, and see yourself as a leader. Remind yourself of why you're capable ("Why *not* me?"), instead of focusing on why you're feeling insecure.

SPOTLIGHT

"My nontraditional path left me feeling unqualified."

When Michelle came to Bossed Up Bootcamp, she was in the running for her dream promotion, the position she'd been working toward for eight years straight with financial services giant American Express.

For the month and a half the position was left open, Michelle's boss told her to "bring it" and prove that she had the leadership chops to step up and fill the shoes of her prior manager, who had moved on to a new post. With so much on the line, Michelle came to Bootcamp hoping for a confidence boost and to gain the skills to demonstrate her leadership potential to her supervisor.

But deep down she worried whether she had what it takes. Was she truly qualified? Could she handle the national responsibilities that came with this new position? If she could, how on earth would she be able to convince her boss that she felt capable, especially when she was still wrestling with her own deep-seated doubts?

At the core of her anxiety was a closely held secret about her nontraditional education. Michelle started working with American Express during her sophomore year of college. It quickly became more than "just a job," and Michelle realized that AMEX offered a real career path. As she rose in the ranks there, Michelle took a break from pursuing her degree to move all over the country as she advanced in the corporate hierarchy, filling roles in Arizona, Utah, and ultimately, in New York City.

As she moved up within AMEX, however, not having completed her degree always concerned her. "Of course I had the experience," Michelle told me, "but I didn't have the credentials. Not going the standard route that most people do chipped away at my confidence."

Michelle ultimately did finish her bachelor's degree part-time while working for AMEX, but not until years after she'd been with the company. Although most of her colleagues didn't know that, the voice in her head calling her capabilities into question was deafening.

I'd be remiss not to mention that Michelle is also a young black woman working in the financial industry, a field not exactly known for its legions of black women in leadership positions. According to 2018 Catalyst data, despite the fact that women make up 45 percent of workers at S&P 500 financial services companies, they only hold 27 percent of executive and senior-level manager positions and constitute a mere 5 percent of the industry's CEOs.[8] Furthermore, when Ursula Burns stepped down as the CEO of Xerox in January 2017, we officially reverted back to having *zero* black women CEOs leading *any* Fortune 500 company.[9]

So when Michelle was staring down the prospect of being promoted into management—the national position she'd been working toward her entire career—it's understandable that she was feeling intimidated.

Michelle decided that, instead of focusing on her insecurities, she would instead ask herself, "Why *not* me?"

"I was technically an analyst at the time," said Michelle, "but I was already doing the work of a manager. Recognizing that was reassuring, and it helped me realize that I could be more assertive with making decisions and leading particular projects forward."

To prove she could be the boss, Michelle started acting like one by taking the lead and more assertively delivering on the projects she was a part of. She made it clear to her director that she was ready for the chance at the promotion and began the formal interview process.

"She offered me the job at the end of the interview," Michelle told me, "and it really took me aback. This moment was eight years in the making and involved so much sacrifice, going back to school, and moving all across the country. It all came flooding into my consciousness and I was overwhelmed."

On the cusp of her twenty-ninth birthday, Michelle gladly stepped into the new role overseeing all of US marketing, services, and change management for American Express. A year and a half later, Michelle would step up yet again, this time into a position with global impact, focusing on change management and large-scale releases for marketing teams.

"It's a new adventure and I'm so proud," Michelle told me.

And as for that voice of doubt? Well, it hasn't gone away, per se.

"It's still playing a part in my day-to-day, but I really make it a conscious effort to question it and say, 'Okay, Michelle, you're here for a reason and people are looking to you for leadership.' "And it helps that the people above, around, and below me really reinforce my leadership, they help keep me honest."

Another coping mechanism that Kramer and Harris recommend for coping with stereotype threat surprised me: jokes!

> By bringing humor to bear on the difficult and stressful situations caused by stereotype threat, women can diminish their negative emotional reactions and increase their performance capabilities. Humor also allows them to change their perspective on the excessive external or internal demands that stereotype threat might otherwise create.
>
> Using humor to cope with stereotype threat is not about laughing out loud, but about cultivating an attitude that gender stereotypes aren't just infuriating, but frequently ridiculous.[10]

I love this! When you're able to laugh at the ridiculousness of sexism, it has less power over you. It's less taxing on your limited energy and internal resources.

I once heard a speaker at a conference share an example of this kind of response from her days as a partner of her law firm. A new client was coming in to discuss his major lawsuit with the partners, and, when she approached him to introduce herself, he asked whether she would be taking him to meet the partners, assuming the young woman before him couldn't possibly be one of them. She laughed, said she would, and then spun 360 degrees on her heels and landed before him once again, extending her hand to shake his. At first, her client was taken aback by the joke, which the attorney then followed swiftly with, "I may not be who you were expecting, but I have a decade more experience in this area of the law than any of my fellow partners here, so I assure you, you're in good hands."

Being able to laugh at the absurdity of it all is not only helpful for staying focused on the task at hand, it helps release stress and anxiety experienced along the way. As presidential speechwriter and *Wall Street Journal* columnist Peggy Noonan once said, "Humor is the shock absorber of life; it helps us take the blows."[11]

Although it is a lifelong challenge to develop and protect your boss identity, focusing on your purpose—your mission, your goals, whatever drives you—will help you maintain your sense of power and agency in your life. Keeping your eye on your end goal keeps you from getting bogged down by the BS we all inevitably run into in our imperfect world.

Focus primarily on your purpose—and *not* how others perceive you—to get stuff done. By taking consistent action in pursuit of your purpose, you'll build up your sense of self-leadership and gain momentum along the way. You'll become the leading lady in your own come-up story. And don't wait for permission to start living this way, because no one else can or will give it to you. Power is not given, it's taken, as Beyoncé says. Only you have the authority to step up and start to *own* your power and in doing so, own your life.

To stay grounded in your purpose, let's start by clarifying your vision for the life and career you want—right now.

Freeing Yourself to Dream Big

Imagine for a second that I waved a magic wand and all your wildest dreams came true. What would your life look like? Where would you be living? Who would you be surrounded by? How would you spend your time? What impact would you be making?

These questions used to be easy for us to answer. When we were just kids on the playground we didn't get bogged down by what was *practical, plausible, or even possible.* We used to dream big without hesitation.

"I want to be an astronaut when I grow up!"

"I want to be president of the United States!"

"I want to be a prima ballerina!"

"I want to be a surgeon and star on Broadway!"

The ambitions we tossed around in playground conversation were more grandiose than grounded in reality. We didn't let those silly details get in the way of our big dreams.

Becoming more practical is a part of growing up. We become more analytical, we gain critical thinking skills, and we learn how to pinpoint the holes in any given plan. As adults, we pride ourselves on bringing logic and reason into arguments. We grownups, it seems, love celebrating the triumph of logic and reason over impracticality.

But one of the innocent bystanders we lose along the way is our imagination. We don't necessarily *want* to lose our ability to dream big as we grow older, but, like so much of our neurology, it's a use-it-or-lose-it-type situation. As we grow older, the triumph of reason means we use our imagination less and less, and those abilities to dream big begin to wither. We start seeing fewer and fewer possibilities for how we could possibly live our lives.

Think back to the wide-open road metaphor I began this chapter with. As we progress in our careers, it's almost as if we see fewer intersections on our chosen path. Once we're deep in the backroads, far off the main highway, we find fewer stop signs along the way and fewer opportunities to change the direction we're headed. This is especially true with the powerful but invisible force of inertia always acting upon us, pushing in the same direction we've already been heading in.

Over time, instead of asking "What do you *want* to do with your life?" or "What do you *want* to learn more about?" we start focusing on "What are you good at?" We go from the courageous act of indulging our curiosity to the risk-averse path of relying on the (supposed) security of what we already know we can do. The issue slowly becomes what you *can* do, not what you *love* to do.

But imaginative thinking isn't just for kids. It's critical for all kinds of innovation, and the most prolific businesses of all time start with an audacious vision. In *Built to Last,* management experts Jim Collins and Jerry Porras reviewed their findings from a longitudinal study of the most successful businesses in our nation's history— and uncovered what characteristics and practices they shared.

One of their key findings was what the authors referred to as BHAGs: Big, Hairy, Audacious Goals.[12] Having a clear, grand vision as a company—despite what seemed practical or even possible— motivates people in a visceral way. It's what gets employees out of bed every morning. BHAGs are big, bold, aspirational, and inspiring. They're typically long-term ambitions (think ten to thirty years into the future) that get people fired up about achieving them.

* In 1909, Henry Ford said, "I'm going to democratize the automobile."
* "We *choose* to go to the moon." That's how President John F. Kennedy introduced the seemingly impossible endeavor way back in 1962.
* "We talked about a computer on every desk and in every home," said Bill Gates, looking back on his early years starting Microsoft.

Clear, compelling, and wildly grandiose ambitions. These are the kinds of visions that Collins and Porras saw in all the companies that were "built to last" over the past century. BHAGs light a fire in your belly—and not just as a business but as someone looking to set *yourself* up for sustainable, long-term success in your career.

Let's give it a try right now. For just a few minutes, suspend your instinct to get analytical and practical. Don't let yourself be bogged down by reason, practicality, or even what you think is *possible*.

Grab a piece of paper or snag my totally free Bossed Up LifeTracker worksheet (the first part of which walks you through this vision exercise) at www.bossedup.com/lifetracker, and write out what your ideal life looks like ten years into the future. Give yourself permission to start there, and know that we'll work backward and leave you with a solid action plan before this book is over. But trust me: before you get to planning, you have to start with *dreaming*.

As you write down your audacious dreams, use the present tense. Imagine yourself ten years in the future, writing a journal entry that's just for you, in which you start each sentence by saying "I'm so happy now that I have . . ." And give yourself ample time to sit in the discomfort of self-exploration. What might start off as an impossibly blurry vision will become easier to see over time, but it may take a bit of experimentation and playfulness to get there.

Think about work. What are you doing every day? What are you getting up and putting on to go to work? Where is work? Who do you work with?

Do you work? Are you making an impact in other ways?

Think about your health and wellness. How is your body feeling? How is your mind? How is your financial wellness? What are you doing just for fun? What are you doing to get moving? What are you eating?

Think about your relationships. Where is your family? How about your friends? How are you spending time together? Are you waking up next to somebody each morning? Are there others in your household?

Now think about anything else we haven't covered. Artistic pursuits? Side hobbies? Travel plans? What else is present in your life that wasn't already covered when thinking about work, wellness, or love and relationships?

Go ahead. Set a timer for ten minutes and write all those out on a piece of paper. I'll wait.

Alright, did you get 'em all out on paper? How does it feel?

"I'm still so unsure. I'm lost. I don't know what I want."

That's okay. Take some pressure off yourself, boss! Are you writing this down in some special notebook or fancy stationery? Toss that aside for now. Go grab the scrappiest scrap piece of paper or back of a napkin that you can find. This is *not* sacred—be playful and flexible with it, not serious and neat.

Now close your eyes, and play pretend. You're ten years into the future, sketch out what you see. Write it all down.

Is that totally stressing you out? Then crumble it up, toss that paper, and do it all over again. Change your entire vision around, if you want. Try on a *totally* different future to see how it feels. Go bigger. Go bolder. Close your eyes again and see it, feel it. Write that one down, too.

Do this as many times as you possibly can in a ten-minute period. Now look for commonalities. What elements stuck around from vision to vision? What changed? How did your body feel with the different visions you came up with? Do some get your heart racing more than others? Read them aloud and see which ones feel right coming out of your mouth. Don't think about which make the most sense—figure out which ones light you up! We'll make sense of all this later, I promise.

———•———

"I couldn't stay in dream mode, I went right into planner mode."

Ah, my fellow Type As—I totally feel you on this! Here's the deal: some of us are very good at the analytical "use your head" part of long-term planning, while others of us are more comfortable with the dreamy "listen to your heart" part of it. To successfully manage long-term goals (which we'll dive *much* deeper into in Chapter 5), you need both your heart and your head engaged.

Your heart is all about those goals that grab you deep down, that get you so excited you can't wait to get to work on them. Your head, thankfully, manages and monitors the heart, helping to steer it in the right direction, step by step, and analyze what's working and what's not working along the way. Some of us lean toward using our heads (me included) and are most swayed by facts and figures, logic and reason. Some of us are much more in tune with our heart—pulled in the direction of our dreams. Sometimes these folks might have a tendency for leaping without looking first, but I got you, boo. We'll work on that.

For now, remember that you must engage both the head and the heart to make long-term, sustainable success possible. So put your to-do-list-loving brain on hold for just a few chapters longer— and, trust me, we will get into planning mode later.

Think of it this way: we're going to chart your course to sustainable success, but we have to point your compass in the right direction first. You will have a road map to getting the sustainable career and life you want by the end of this book, but, before we get into action, take the lead and point yourself in the direction you want to go.

———•———

"I'm totally intimidated. What did I just commit to?! Ah!"

Also totally normal! I call this "vision vertigo." It's like you're standing atop a huge mountain looking down and thinking, "Holy shit! How on earth did I get up here?!"

Having big, lofty goals can be intimidating. But that discomfort is a sign that you're venturing into territory that's on your growth edge. That's an uncomfortable but excellent zone to be in right now. Don't worry, we're going to get right into practical, tactical ways for you to start breaking down these big dreams into manageable action steps in the chapters ahead.

Setting big, hairy, audacious goals can leave you feeling that pang of fear in your stomach right around now, too.

What if I don't make this happen?

What if I can't?

What if I fail?

Those anxieties are perfectly normal, especially if you've been comfortably cruising along for years, pushed along by inertia keeping you on the same exact path you've been on.

I like to think of Jim Carrey's wise words from a commencement address he gave at Maharishi University in 2014. In it, he told the story of his father, who was a talented comedian but never pursued it professionally. Instead, he did what he figured was the safe, responsible thing: he became an accountant. Later on, he was laid off, and that "safe" path turned out to be much less reliable than he thought it would be. Jim's family went through some tough years, but his father taught him a tremendously valuable lesson that would later push him to pursue acting and comedy: "You can fail at what you don't want, so you might as well take a chance on doing what you love."

So many of us choose our path out of fear disguised as practicality. What we really want seems impossibly out of reach and ridiculous to expect, so we never dare to ask the universe for it.[13]

Dare to ask for it, boss.

Sure, there are risks in pursuing your dream career and life. But you *also* face quieter, more invisible risks by not pursuing them. You risk never knowing what opportunities were waiting for you, had you only tried.

YOU CAN FAIL AT WHAT YOU
DON'T WANT, SO YOU MIGHT AS
WELL TAKE A CHANCE
*on doing what
you love.*

JIM CARREY

With that in mind, I want you to look back at the vision for your life and career that you wrote down and answer these two simple questions:

- ✴ **What makes you uniquely equipped to fulfill this vision?** Your audacious vision is not arbitrary—it's yours for a reason. Why?
- ✴ **What do you need to learn to get there?** What is it that you don't know yet but will have to figure out?

That curiosity will carry you forward with the calm confidence you need to see this adventure through. And let me be clear: following your curiosity is different from blindly "following your passion." Elizabeth Gilbert got it right in her book *Big Magic,* in which she railed against this useless bit of advice:

> If someone has a clear passion, odds are they're already following it and they don't need anyone to tell them to pursue it. (That's kind of the definition of passion, after all: an interest that you chase obsessively, almost because you have no choice.) But a lot of people don't know exactly what their passion is, or they may have multiple passions, or they may be going through a midlife change of passion—all of which can leave them feeling confused and blocked and insecure.[14]

She's right. I'm not advocating that you simply "follow your passion." I'm asking you to play with it a little. Let it marinate. Swirl it around in your wineglass with your besties. Give it some airtime over dinner with the boo. Daydream out loud and in your most private of journals. Dream on it. Scheme on it.

SPOTLIGHT

"I thought I didn't have any passion."

Maggie joined us at Bossed Up Bootcamp back in 2015, when she knew that she could no longer continue on at her day job. At twenty-seven, she'd spent nearly five years working for an international nonprofit organization and had just received her second promotion, but she couldn't shake the feeling that something was missing.

It came to a head when she and her partner, Dan, were heading to a friend's wedding. She boarded the plane and promptly had a total meltdown. Sobbing in her window seat, she started questioning everything she was doing with her life.

"I was asking myself, '*Was this it?*'" Maggie recalled. "I felt like all my life choices had been keeping me content and comfortable, but would they lead to happiness? I didn't think so."

She felt disconnected from her passion and purpose, and, frankly, she didn't even know what those were anymore. Making matters worse, Maggie was convinced that her friends and colleagues all had it figured out. "It seemed like everyone else had settled into their careers and lives by now, and here I was, questioning the path I'd been on my entire career."

She fell into a true depressive state and at one point even wondered whether perhaps she wasn't *meant* to be happy. Frustrated and feeling lost, Maggie wondered, "Why can't I just be grateful for what I have?"

At Bootcamp, Maggie did the vision exercise in the prompts I walked you through in the previous few pages. "It was excruciating," Maggie told me. "I felt like everyone knew what they wanted to do except me. I thought I didn't have any passion."

But in the critical few months that followed, Maggie allowed herself to follow her curiosity and start taking action outside her comfort zone anyway. She found herself drawn to feminist organizations and sought out opportunities to make a meaningful impact. She joined multiple women's community groups and even started volunteering with a local abortion fund organization, answering calls from women who were struggling to find the funds to pay for the procedure.

She began noticing a common theme among all the women she was connecting with: women were stressed, confused, and anxious about money.

"I've always considered personal finance a nerdy hobby of mine," said Maggie, "and financial literacy came easily to me. So it was only natural that I offered to help the women I was meeting, whether that meant creating a budget template or a debt payment plan."

The more she offered help, the more she felt the satisfaction of making a direct positive impact on the lives of the women she was supporting. It ignited a fire inside her, boosted her confidence, and for the first time caused her to consider making a go at financial coaching.

But, up until then, Maggie had been defined in her career as a nonprofit advocate, a team player embedded in an enormous international institution. What on earth would make *her* feel qualified to hang her own shingle in a totally different industry?

Despite her doubts, she continued taking deliberate actions in the direction of her dreams. A full six months after she'd started exploring making a career change, Maggie took on her first financial coaching client—and charged her nothing. "I'm not a risk taker by nature. I'm not an obvious entrepreneur," said Maggie, "but I was amazed at the rapid improvements I was seeing in my clients' and friends' finances. It became clear that I was having a real impact."

So, without quitting her day job, Maggie followed her curiosity further and pursued a certificate in financial education instruction. Wanting to support her clients in making mindset shifts around money, she also started a six-month coaching certification program.

Maggie stayed focused on her purpose and allowed herself to explore how she might make the impact she desired and help more women take charge of their money. That required *not* worrying too much about the perception others might have of her straying "off path" from her career in the nonprofit sector.

Over time, Maggie's confidence and identity as a financial coach were bolstered by her clients' results. "As my clients began to see *themselves* differently, pay off debt, get higher-paying jobs, and negotiate effectively," said Maggie, "it helped me see *myself* differently. It helped me feel deeply impactful and made me more confident about making this my career."

Just about two years after she'd first had that panic attack on the plane, Maggie officially quit her day job and launched her own financial coaching business, where to this day she helps women gain control over their finances.

"My passion had been there all along," said Maggie, "I just needed to give myself the time, space, and permission to explore it."

Let your curiosity guide you, and make your vision something you tease out over time. Just like your leadership identity, clarifying your vision is an iterative process. It gets stronger, more audacious, and more powerful the more you give it a go.

—— • ——

By now I hope you're thinking about how to set your sights on a career path that you would love and feel a renewed sense of possibility in pursuing it. Because your vision and boss identity both require iteration, the potential for failure on the road to long-term sustainable success is a real possibility.

In the next chapter, we'll talk about how to focus on progress—not perfection—when getting bossed up, and how you can still keep your big, audacious ambitions alive even when facing inevitable setbacks along the way.

Chapter 3

Progress over Perfection

Now that you've set some big audacious goals and started to see yourself as the lead character in the story of achieving them, it's important to acknowledge the equally important counterpart to big-time ambition: resilience.

I wish it were as simple as stepping into your power, aiming high, and making the leap, but sustainable success isn't achieved in a linear fashion. It comes in fits and starts. Two steps forward, one step back. Failures are inevitable on the road to success; it's *how you deal with them* that shapes your outcomes.

If you think about it, our culture almost exclusively celebrates starters and finishers. Parents proudly post videos to social media of their fourth grader beaming over her first rendition of "Mary Had a Little Lamb" on the violin. When that fourth grader performs at Carnegie Hall decades later, her world erupts into applause once again. But those years of sweating over her stringed instrument in between? There is rarely an audience for that. No applause. No praise. And very few Facebook likes.

Our culture celebrates starting something new and reaching the peaks of success. But we often overlook the necessary—though far less glamorous—muddling through the middle, where the real magic happens.

When Goals Crush You (Instead of the Other Way Around)

I found this out firsthand when I started Bossed Up back in 2013. At the time, I'd been dreaming and sketching out the ideas behind Bossed Up for the better part of a year. I started speaking my vision out loud, as it happens, while stretching outside my comfort zone in a totally different arena: training for my first-ever half marathon with a group of running buddies. I never considered myself a runner, so when I thought about running 13.1 miles—a ludicrous, lofty goal—I knew I needed to team up with more experienced runners. Fortunately, DC has no shortage of them. Before long I found myself meeting up each Saturday morning with a new pack of running buddies and hitting new personal records! I witnessed in a visceral way what it looked like to break down a giant, seemingly impossible goal into manageable steps. Through these concrete actions, I was expanding my very identity and starting to see myself as a "runner" for the first time.

It was on these runs that I also workshopped my ideas for Bossed Up, the company that was brewing in my mind, and met my first business partner, Simone. Simone took me out for coffee, after a few weeks of me going on and on about the business plan I was putting in place and the research I was devouring in preparation for launch, and she asked me whether she could be a part of it. She was in law school, an experienced manager in a male-dominated field, and had financial resources to spare, all of which were resources she could bring to the table that I couldn't. It didn't take long before we had drafted up our 50/50 equity agreement and filed the business together.

We were off to the races. It was just as exciting as the first day I ran ten miles. Double digits! I never thought I'd see the day. Hot damn!

Starting the business was thrilling. We took fancy headshots, commissioned my friends and recent design school grads Lyndse and Ellie to design us a killer logo (and I'm proud to say we're still working with them to this day), and I pulled together a scrappy but functional website. We started identifying trainers and topics for our very first training—Bossed Up Bootcamp—and, with a little money pushing some Facebook ads, we had our first sales rolling in. This was real cold hard cash, baby! With my business plan in hand and some savings squirrelled away in my bank account, I quit my consulting job. I was all in! I had made the leap and *everything was so exciting!*

See, starting stuff is pretty dope. People love starting things. I got *all the Facebook likes!*

Then, a few things happened. First, I filed my taxes and realized I owed thousands more than I'd initially thought. That final year before quitting my fat-cat consulting job I'd made more money than ever before. But there's a funny thing about that: it meant I owed more than ever before. Go figure. All of a sudden my already modest financial safety net was cut in half.

Immediately after our first Bossed Up Bootcamp, Simone and I promptly got a tad drunk to celebrate our success. *Clink* Yay! We were on cloud nine, or so it seemed. So you can imagine my surprise when the next day, the very next conversation we had ultimately led to our business lady divorce (the technical term is "dissociation," but it sure as shit felt like a divorce). It boiled down to this: only through *doing the work* did we realize that we had radically different visions for Bossed Up's future. I didn't quit my job to radically compromise on my business vision, so I stood my ground. Simone was understandably frustrated by this, to the point where it was hard to see a path forward in which both our visions could peacefully coexist within a single corporate entity. We signed the papers a week later, and, the next day, we left for a vacation together in Maine. Despite the end of our corporate relationship, we didn't want our friendship to bite the dust, too. We spent a week in Bar Harbor destressing and processing what had just happened together, but our relationship just wasn't the same. We existed in totally different worlds. She still had her six-figure consulting job, and I was wondering how I could even begin to move forward with a fledgling company all on my own.

Within the terms of our amicable but sad separation, we divvied up all the assets of our little infant company. That meant writing Simone a check for 50 percent of everything in the Bossed Up bank account at the time. It also meant I was just about broke. Again. Everything we poured into Bossed Up for the past few months, everything I risked to do so, amounted to nothing. Well, not *nothing* nothing, but certainly not enough to keep me going financially. So I did what I had to do: I got a job. A full-time job. Any job I could find. Fortunately, it didn't take me long to find a political campaign in need of my digital skills; it just meant packing my bags, kissing the still relatively new boo farewell, and heading across the country to beautiful Portland, Oregon.

Everything I'd been planning, everything I'd done, felt like it might as well have never happened. I felt like I had nothing to show for it. Bossed Up was a shell—a facade. I felt, like a huge failure. I was lost, alone, and afraid. And that's *while* being fortunate enough to still have a roof over my head and a reliable paycheck coming in again. Life did not feel invigorating. There were no Facebook likes. I was worried that people would judge me as a flop. "Wait—didn't you start that thing, Bossed Up? What the hell are you doing out in Portland?"

But here's a funny thing: no one cares as much as you do. No one means any harm by it, either, they're just not as preoccupied with the trials and tribulations of your life as you are. It's okay. Don't take it personally. It's actually great, in a way, because it means you don't need to announce every major hiccup you run into. You can choose to lie low while you're navigating the turbulent parts of your journey, and that's okay.

Truthfully, I could have quit Bossed Up right then. It would not have been hard. It felt like that was the direction I was headed anyway. It was the path of least resistance. It would have been a tad embarrassing, but it would be over and done with, and I could move on. Playing double duty with a day job *and* my fledgling startup occupying my nights and weekends wasn't easy, especially after those precious first three months of working on Bossed Up full time. I felt like I was missing out. I desperately wanted my time back to focus exclusively on Bossed Up! But I knew I couldn't burn out again on my quest to help others banish burnout—the irony would be too rich. So I had to learn to pace myself and for once in my life have patience with the process.

There were lots of tears. Lots of heartache. Lots of doubt. Should I have parted ways with Simone? Should I have just started solo from the start? Where do I go from here? I was full of angst and fear.

But, in the face of all that, something about this work felt . . . almost inevitable. Like I was being pulled toward pursuing this company. I was so aligned with its core mission, I couldn't keep myself away. My heart was pulling me in that direction, despite the fact that I didn't know how to take the next step. I made the conscious choice to get back up, brush my shoulders off, and keep going in whatever ways I could. I was committed to making my vision a reality and realized it was going to take time to grow Bossed Up in the way I wanted to. I would end up working full time while slowly growing Bossed Up on the side for the entire next year.

What kept me going in those darkest of days? Two things, really. First, a calm confidence in my ability to *figure it out*. I didn't know what I didn't know, but I was pretty sure that I could learn it. I could handle it. I'd survived worse! The second was the realization that I wasn't alone in this, after all. Not only did I have the unshakeable faith of Brad the boo and my early-adopter Bossed Up community members fueling my confidence, but there were plenty of others who wanted to see Bossed Up happen, too! But I realized that *I* needed to reach out to *them*, because they weren't going to make it a priority until I asked them. It was during this time that I assembled our advisory board (a formal term for how I roped in my most accomplished friends, mentors, and people I had a total career crush on, to serve in a volunteer supervisory capacity).

Assembling the advisory board was easily the best business decision I'd made thus far, and it resulted in gaining this sage advice from my friend and mentor who was an accomplished entrepreneur herself, in the midst of starting her second company: She reminded me that the launch is scary, but it's exhilarating. It's the startup slog that follows that causes most businesses to fail. That's the part where you're taking your proof of concept and figuring out how to operationalize it for the long term. I just needed to make it through the slog. And, truly, everyone has to deal with the slog when setting out on a challenging long-term goal—not just entrepreneurs.

And guess what? The slog is where all the good stuff happens.

Pivot or Persevere?

It was during this time that I thought back to *The Lean Startup*, by Eric Ries, one of the books I'd read as I prepared to launch Bossed Up and solidified our business plan.[1] Although the book is intended for entrepreneurs, I've found these principles just as applicable for anyone navigating a big life change and setting out to achieve a big goal.

The best lesson I took away from it—and one that I firmly believe applies to all of our lives and careers—was this: Don't run from what's not working. Instead, take a closer look, analyze what you know and don't know, and come up with theories that you can test to find out more. Is the business model not working because your pricing is off? Is your career transition stuck because you're lacking experience on Capitol Hill? Are you injured because you're approaching half-marathon training the wrong way? Try to drill down on a variable you can adjust and experiment with. Then decide: Do I pivot my strategy or persevere the same way? Do I go in a different direction, or do I try again?

I love this language because it takes the negative connotation behind "quitting" and reframes it as "pivoting." This makes a *whole lot* more sense to me, because sometimes quitting is absolutely the best option. I know this is an odd position to take in a chapter on resilience, but it's true! In one of my favorite podcast episodes ever, from the *Freakonomics* team, titled "The Upside of Quitting,"[2] host Stephen Dubner explains, "Sometimes quitting is strategic, and sometimes it can be your best possible plan." He highlighted the fact that "sunk costs"—or all that time, effort, money, and resources you've already poured into a project—can cloud your judgment and cause you to continue on in blind pursuit of a goal, even if that goal no longer serves you. What you must consider alongside your sunk costs, argues Dubner, are your "opportunity costs," or what other opportunities you may be passing up while you're in pursuit of that initial goal. In other words, would your focus, energy, money, or time be better spent elsewhere? Don't keep heading down a path just because it's the path you started down.

The other reason I love the "pivot or persevere" framework is because pivoting doesn't mean quitting *forever*. It just means you might no longer be focusing on that particular strategy because your time and energy need to be redirected. It's simply a shift in direction. It's not the end of the pursuit. That's what getting a day job felt like for me: a tacit acceptance that I could either raise startup investor funds (something I wanted to avoid) or find a way to keep paying my bills through another job while figuring out a sustainable business model that would work for me.

When you decide to persevere—to continue on and try again—failure provides an opportunity to proceed more intelligently. Sometimes in the midst of the pain, anger, frustration, and sadness that come with messing up big-time, we forget to look for the bright spots. Even when something tanks, there's always *some* component that we can learn from. So start by considering this:

What *is* working and how do I replicate that? And, on the flip side, what's *not* working and needs to be adjusted when I try again?

When you focus on what you learned, you flip failure on its head. You make it work for you.

SPOTLIGHT

"My challenges made me who I am."

After starting off her career in NYC and rising rapidly in finance and media, Tiffany was craving the opportunity to create something new. So she landed a job at an early stage startup that combined her passion for community building and her desire to be part of the tech scene. She moved across the country, leaving her friends and network behind, to establish the San Francisco office for a new co-living company.

At first it seemed her new position would be a creative, entrepreneurial endeavor. But, just a few months in, Tiffany started to worry that the job was less about building community and more about sales and logistics. This wasn't what she'd hoped for, but Tiffany continued to work hard nonetheless, not wanting to look like a whiner.

But life was about to deal Tiffany a double whammy. First, she was assaulted on the street on her way in to work one day. In a total state of shock, Tiffany was mainly concerned with making the morning team conference call. So by the time she called the police at her boss's urging, the operator berated her for not calling sooner and asked, "Do you really think we're gonna catch this guy now? It's been forty-five minutes."

A few short months later, Tiffany was shocked to learn that she was being let go. Despite her top sales numbers, positive affirmation from her direct reports, and her unanswered requests for formal feedback from her manager, they were firing her. Tiffany filed a formal complaint and even missed out on severance pay because she refused to sign their requisite NDA. More than a year later, her investigation is still ongoing.

Feeling rejected and isolated, and on the other side of the country from her friends and loved ones, Tiffany was at a loss. But she was no stranger to setbacks. At the age of nine Tiffany and her family were in a devastating car accident. Her father did not survive, and she suffered multiple broken bones in her leg and a nerve injury that resulted in the permanent loss of movement in her right arm.

Living with disability left Tiffany even more motivated to excel academically. "I was always being told about my limitations, about things I'd never be able to do," said Tiffany, "but applying myself to my schoolwork was something I could control, so I focused there."

Tiffany went on to achieve high marks throughout her education, started off her career as an investment banker ranked at the top of her peer group, and worked at two global media companies before taking the co-living startup role.

So when Tiffany found herself fired and unsure of where to take her career next, she thought back to all she'd overcome in the past and had confidence in her ability to triumph over these new challenges as well.

Working through her shock and grief in therapy, Tiffany soon recognized that her desire to create something new didn't necessarily need to be fulfilled by working on someone else's startup. In fact, Tiffany had already started her own advocacy group, Diversability, back in college and had established it as a nonprofit when living in NYC. Diversability was dedicated to fostering community among disabled people that wasn't rooted in pity and tragedy, but rather focused on empowerment and pride. She'd kept it running on the side all these years by hiring someone else to handle day-to-day operations, but that person had just moved on from the organization. This was it, Tiffany realized. This was her moment to pivot and give her own startup her full attention.

"I never started Diversability to do this full time," Tiffany confessed, "because I think real inclusion is having a disability and being in the mainstream workforce. Your very presence is your advocacy. So although I loved it, I'd never imagined working on diversity issues full time."

But, when she finally gave herself permission to develop a new vision for her career, she was off to the races. With all Tiffany had learned from her experience in finance, media, and the startup world, she was well equipped to take Diversability to the next level. She established a speakers' bureau for speakers with disabilities. and helped connect conferences and corporations with them while negotiating their compensation agreements. She started a micro-grant funding initiative to provide financing for other activists in the disability space. Shortly after stepping up as full-time CEO, Tiffany was invited to be a part of filming a TV series with Harvard professor Michael Sandel, was featured in *Marie Claire* magazine, and was invited to speak at Davos for the World Economic Forum.

"Watching Diversability grow is almost parallel with my own journey to becoming comfortable in my own skin," said Tiffany. "It started as a side project—something I really didn't think to do full time, kind of like my disability was something I didn't want to deal with."

But in some ways, the setbacks, uncertainty, and trauma Tiffany experienced made her who she is today. "Turns out, this thing I didn't want to define me is actually a huge part of who I am, and now I'm seeing that manifest in my work and in how I'm continuing to evolve and grow. I'm still a work in progress, but my ultimate goal is to create as much access and opportunity for people in the disability community as possible."

A Few Good "Failures"

The more I studied it, the more I realized that failure is inevitable on the road to success.

No one is a true overnight success—that's just oversimplified marketing designed to appeal to our love of starters and finishers. In reality, there are some very famous "failures" among us.

Michael Jordan, for instance, failed to make his high school basketball team. Can you imagine? Think back to something you totally tanked in high school. How did it impact you? Jordan went home, locked himself in his bedroom, and cried. That's certainly how failure felt to me in high school (and, who am I kidding, it still does today). But, after he dried his eyes, Jordan became

**FAILURE IS INEVITABLE
ON THE ROAD**
to success

EMILIE ARIES

near-obsessive with his practice, a habit that he carried with him through his NBA glory days. Phil Jackson, former coach of the Chicago Bulls, said that Michael Jordan simply practiced with greater concentration and drive than anyone else. He would work himself "into a lather" with his intensity and push himself harder when things got difficult. Even when he was the premier player in the game, Jordan rarely took a day off from his demanding practice routine. "No matter how good you are," Jordan famously said, "always keep working on your game."

You might not know Wilma Rudolph's name quite as well, but she was once the fastest woman on the planet after becoming the first American woman to win three gold medals at one Olympic Games. In the 1960 Rome Olympics, she placed first in the track-and-field, sprint, and relay contests. I was surprised to learn that she didn't exactly hit the ground running in her time here on earth, however. She was born premature, weighing only 4.5 pounds, the twentieth of twenty-two children born to her parents (nope, that's not a typo). At four years old, she nearly died after battling pneumonia, scarlet fever, and polio, which left her left leg mostly paralyzed. Doctors warned her parents that she might never have the use of her left leg again, but for eight years little Wilma diligently pursued physical therapy until she learned to walk normally without a leg brace at twelve. She joined her high school's basketball team and started running in track-and-field races shortly thereafter. She lost *every single race* in the first official track meet she entered, but she wasn't deterred. Looking back on her unlikely and illustrious career, Wilma said, "I just want to be remembered as a hardworking lady."

Although sports do provide some helpful metaphors, such "failures" aren't limited to the athletic world. Oprah was demoted in one of her early jobs on daytime network TV. Vera Wang began her career as a competitive figure skater and only began exploring fashion after failing to make the 1968 Olympic figure skating team. J. K. Rowling wrote the first Harry Potter book as a struggling single mother while receiving welfare benefits, and she faced twelve rejections from publishers before finally selling the first book for only $4,000.

Having real role models who are willing to share their full story—the good, the bad, and the ugly—is so critical to keeping your head on straight when shit hits the fan. But, in our culture that worships the "naturally gifted" and the myth of overnight success, these tales of true grit can be hard to come by on the happy hour circuit or in the day-to-day networking game. And certainly on social media. That's part of the reason I'm so obsessed with Jessica Bacal's book, *Mistakes I Made at Work,* subtitled *25 Influential Women Reflect on What They Got Out of Getting It Wrong.*

It's both comforting and awe inspiring to read these short vignettes from accomplished women who dare to bare all—and, no, I'm not talking about going makeup-free to some cover shoot. These are real-life stories of the power of perseverance contributed by writers, leaders, innovators, and policy makers.

One story from Bacal's collection was from Judith Warner, a distinguished author and *New York Times* columnist. She beautifully articulated this very Bossed Up gem:

> When you're caught up in external signs of success, you don't necessarily take care of yourself in ways that lead to personal sustainability. This undermines resilience because at a certain point you crash and burn.[3]

Resilience isn't about ignoring your stumbles and obsessing over your successes; it's about learning from them both. It's about seeing yourself as someone who is ever evolving, on a journey to becoming better and better—through hard work and practice. Such "failures" as Michael Jordan, Wilma Rudolph, Oprah, Vera Wang, J. K. Rowling, and any of the many brilliant people who have failed on their way to the top can help remind all of us that even on our darkest days, we're a work in progress.

The Struggle Is Not Real

Looking back on all the struggle I faced in Bossed Up's first few years, I can't help but laugh. I know old Emilie would want to smack me for chuckling over what felt like the end of the world back then, but it seems silly now how much I stressed over my stumbles. In reality, what I was gaining was a boatload of learning. How else was I supposed to figure this stuff out? Trial and error can be a priceless teacher. But those dark days of the slog aren't easy to celebrate. They aren't even that easy to tolerate, primarily because of the stories we tell ourselves about failure.

"I'm just not good at public speaking."

"I'm not a born leader."

"I don't know anything about running a business."

"Maybe I'm just not as smart as I thought I was."

"I'm not cut out for this."

I still catch myself falling into mental dead-ends like these. When you believe in that simple binary—you either have what it takes or you don't—there's not much to be done about it. This mental snag belies a way of thinking that's ingrained in us from a very young age.

Researcher Carol Dweck calls this a "fixed trait mindset."[4] It means that you believe there are certain fundamental skills and talents innate to *who you are*. Of course this also means you believe there are shortcomings innate to who you are, too. You're either smart or you're not. You're either a savvy businesswoman or you're not. You're a born leader or you're not. There are certain skills that you just aren't meant for—things you'll never be able to do.

For the logically oriented like me, you might be thinking . . . *well, yeah!* I'm not going to become a prolific track star at the age of ninety, so of course this is true! (You might first want to google "Olga Kotelko" before you rule anything out for sure, though.)

But going about our daily lives with the underlying belief that there are certain things we're good at and certain things we're bad at is not nearly as innocuous as it seems. In fact, it can have a profound and debilitating impact on our growth potential.

Dweck and her researchers ran studies among fifth graders to see what impact a fixed trait mindset might have, as opposed to a "growth mindset," which presumes that, no matter who you are, you can always become smarter or more skilled through hard work and effort.

Researchers gave two groups of students a series of puzzles, starting with easy ones, and gradually moving on to more difficult ones. Along the way, researchers either praised students on their intelligence ("You're very good at this; you must be very smart") or on their effort ("You're very good at this; you must have worked hard"). The students praised for their intelligence were, in effect, prompted to have a fixed trait mindset. They saw their achievement as a result of their innate intelligence and abilities. Those praised for their hard work were primed into a growth mindset, because they credited their achievement to effort.

Interesting differences emerged when the puzzles got harder. The students with a fixed trait mindset lost confidence and were quickly discouraged when faced with difficulty. When asked to explain their hardship, students said things like, "I'm just not very good at this." When given the choice, the fixed trait students were more likely to choose to go back to doing the easier puzzles they had already completed than to move on to the more difficult, new puzzles.

The students with a growth mindset reacted quite differently to the challenge. They saw difficulty as a sign of progress and learning. When given the choice, they were much more likely to opt for the harder puzzles, because they actually *feel smarter* when they're working really hard on something difficult.

Having a growth mindset enables you to stay actively engaged in the learning process, even when faced with setbacks. It means you're better equipped to "get curious, not furious" in the face of mistakes. To me, this is not only better for your mental health; it's also just plain productive. It means that even the biggest curveballs won't throw you off your game entirely.

It also means you're more likely to stay engaged in and actually learn from your failures. Dweck found that students with a growth mindset had higher measurable brain activity when faced with failure than their fixed trait mindset counterparts, who had tuned out and shut down completely. Why? The growth mindset kids were trying to figure out *where they went wrong*. They were troubleshooting!

**HAVE CONFIDENCE
IN YOUR ABILITY**

to figure it out.

EMILIE ARIES

Having a growth mindset means believing in the power of hard work and practice. It means having faith that anyone can learn and grow and get smarter. As I like to say, have confidence in your ability to figure it out.

Ironically, developing a growth mindset requires a certain amount of emotional detachment from your work. Even though you're a dedicated, hardworking person who takes pride in your efforts, a growth mindset requires having a healthy distance between *who you are* and *what you do*. It's the difference between "I fucked up" and "I *am* a fuck-up." It means, when a project fails, when you don't get the second interview, or when tragedy strikes, you don't internalize the outcome. The outcome is not *equal to you* in value. You are not what you do. In other words: even when you fail, you are *worthy*.

Having a fixed trait mindset looks quite different. If you fundamentally believe that your achievements are a reflection of your core skills and traits, then your entire self-worth is in jeopardy in the face of failure! If "I did well on the exam" translates to "I *am* smart," then of course you're going to run from poor outcomes like your entire personhood is under attack. That's quite a burden to live with. It means you feel under constant pressure to prove to yourself and others that your traits—being smart, being a good writer, being a straight-A student, whatever—are immutable.

So what does that mean, in practice? Well, Dweck and her research team found that those with a fixed trait mindset are more prone to cheating to get the outcomes they desire (like a good score on a test, for instance). They are also more likely to decline a challenge and become risk averse. If you live your life in constant fear of failure, you're prone to stop seeking out new challenges and, in turn, stop learning. Imagine living your life constantly doing the same puzzles over and over again, afraid to try the harder ones. It's how a lot of us live.

I'm reminded of Beyoncé's wise words on perfectionism: "If everything was perfect you would never learn and you would never grow."

It's not easy to adopt a growth mindset, but it can be done! Here's how to start:

1. Celebrate Effort over Achievement

That ten-year vision you started to articulate in the previous chapter can feel intimidating—and it's supposed to! That's a vision of a life and career you would *love,* but it's not intended to be achievable overnight. To sustain your drive and motivation, keep tabs on the effort and hard work you're putting in to make it a reality. Even if you fail to meet the specific achievements you'd hoped for as quickly as you'd planned, acknowledging the effort you're putting in will make you less likely to become discouraged in the face of setbacks. You'll bounce back faster when you focus on the hard work—not just the outcome.

One way to develop this mindfulness further is to flip the script on daily to-do lists by writing down everything you do each day as you accomplish each task. Instead of writing down all the things you still have left to do, you'll focus on everything you achieve each day and, in doing so, keep tabs on your progress. At the end of the week, even though there's always going to be more work on the horizon, you'll be able to look back at your long list of things you tackled throughout the course of the week and feel a sense of forward momentum.

2. Redirect Your Inner Dialogue

One of the realities of big, audacious goals is that you're going to stumble on the road to making them a reality. How we judge ourselves at our highest highs and lowest lows can play a crucial role in maintaining our confidence. What are you telling yourself when things go well or go poorly?

Say a negotiation with your boss goes awry, for instance, and you catch the voice in your head saying, "That did not go well, I am a terrible negotiator." Instead, redirect it to tell a new story—one from a growth mindset perspective that acknowledges the effort you did (or didn't) put into it. "That did not go well. I wish I'd actually done those role-playing exercises, or learned more about what budget my boss has to work with before I had that conversation."

Redirecting your inner narrative is just as important when things *do* go well. When you're crushin' your goals, don't climb onto the "I'm such hot shit!" bravado bandwagon. You may be feeling like a million bucks, but remember that it's your hard work and effort that got you there—not some innate skill you were born with. Understanding *what you did* that made things go so well will help you replicate that recipe for success in the future, too.

3. Differentiate Between What You Do and Who You Are

Instead of internalizing difficulty as a reflection of your own personal deficiencies, see challenge as evidence of learning. Let's say you've set a goal to run your first 5K by next month, but you find yourself walking through most of it on race day with the voices in your head saying, "I just can't run. I'm just not athletic. I'll never be a healthy person." Those fixed trait mindset voices chip away at your boss identity because they confuse who you are with what you did (or didn't do).

Adopting a growth mindset acknowledges the power you have to take purposeful action next time—to practice more, to change up your routine, to find a running buddy, to start tracking your day-to-day training regimen.

What you achieve is not who you are. Period. Write it down and say it out loud if you have to.

———•———

Changing your mindset, just like cultivating your boss identity, is a process that takes time. But it's also one of those things that once you learn about it, it's hard to *not* see growth mindset and fixed trait mindset speech everywhere you turn!

SPOTLIGHT

"I jumped out of the sky—I can do anything!"

Heather has always been a planner. A pro/con list maker, a task-master extraordinaire, Heather is someone who always looks before she leaps. She absolutely adores the Gallup Strengths-finder test, which determined that "strategy" was her strongest personality trait.

"In my first job out of college," Heather told me, "I had five specific goals that I wanted to achieve while there. It took me five years, but I did it! And I wasn't going to move on until I had."

It was right around that time that Heather's dear friend invited her to celebrate her thirtieth birthday—with a skydiving trip. Heather said she was in from the start, but, as someone who suffers from vertigo, she was in disbelief as the words "I'll do it!" came out of her mouth.

"The worst part was signing all my rights away," said Heather. "There was all this talk in the contract about not suing in case of death or near death, and I'm thinking to myself, '*What on earth am I doing?*'"

It turns out, all the other pals who initially said they were in had bailed, and Heather didn't want to be another flake. She was going to push past her fear, she decided, and try not to overthink things for a change. She was all strapped in and ready for her tandem jump with an instructor and watched as the small plane they were in climbed higher and higher. Her instructor screamed into her ear, "Okay, you open the door now."

"*What?!*" thought Heather, "*I have to do it myself?!*"

It turns out, if she didn't open the door, she didn't jump. It was company policy. Heather took a deep breath, summoned strength from an unknown reservoir, and reached out to swing the plane door open.

"Okay, now you have to swing your legs over the edge," shouted her instructor.

Again, moving as though she were in a dream, Heather saw herself edging her body off the side of the plane. It was terrifying, but she suddenly found herself recognizing a sense of exhilaration, too.

"Those three minutes of free fall that followed were some of the best minutes of my life," Heather told me. "Still today I remember how I felt just pure bliss, despite being so out of control. It was life changing."

When her feet hit the ground and Heather realized she had, in fact, remained intact and alive, she shouted into the sky, "I'm a *badass*!" and thought to herself, "I jumped out of the sky—I can do *anything*!"

In the months that followed, Heather started to think of herself differently. She was still proud to be strategic, sure, but she was also the kind of woman who jumped out of a dang airplane! This experience expanded what she thought of herself and what she considered *possible* for herself.

So she decided to leave her job and relocate to DC, without anything lined up—a totally uncharacteristic move for Heather! But, after five years working in development for a small liberal arts college in western New York State, she was craving a more cosmopolitan, international crowd. With a newfound sense of her own ability to learn through risk taking, for once in her life she didn't feel the need to have a plan worked out before she made her next move.

She crashed at a friend's place outside the city while she started her job search in earnest. She began working nights at a pizza joint to help defray costs while she applied for multiple jobs every day. When Heather started to feel the pangs of anxiety and depression creeping in on her, she did something also totally outside of her comfort zone: she got a Groupon and signed up for belly dancing classes.

To be clear: Heather had absolutely no prior dance experience whatsoever. In fact, dance was considered a mortal sin in the religious tradition that Heather was brought up in as a child, so this was not something she expected to be good at. But that's not what she was trying to get out of her newfound hobby! Rather, she appreciated that the classes were more affordable than therapy, gave her a boost of feel-good endorphins, provided some semblance of a routine, and got her out of the house and into an environment where she might meet some new people. Still today some of Heather's closest friends in DC are women she met through those classes.

In the meantime, Heather's expanding growth mindset was impacting her job search as well. At the start, she was applying for jobs that were exactly like what she'd been doing previously: fundraising and development roles in institutions of higher education. In other words, Heather was opting for the same puzzles she'd been solving for years. But, with her newfound confidence, she started to expand her scope: after all, how else would she learn what she might be good at if she continued working in the same environments and in the same roles year after year? So she broadened her search to other kinds of non-profit organizations and roles for which she felt a bit less qualified. Heather started actively seeking out a position that would challenge her to learn and grow.

"It wasn't because I was getting desperate either," Heather told me. "I'd simply realized that *I* had been holding myself back by limiting my search to jobs I was sure I'd be *good* at. But how could I know I *wouldn't* be good at something if I didn't at least explore it?"

Heather started to approach her job search as a grand adventure. Each application was like trying on a costume of who she might want to become.

"It was actually *fun* instead of stressful!" said Heather. "And that must have been coming through in my cover letters and applications because all of a sudden I was getting a lot more calls and interviews."

Heather forced herself to show up for interviews even when she didn't feel perfectly qualified by telling herself she was just exploring and "playing dress-up" with her career. It took the nerves away, and her interviews continued to improve.

Just over four months after moving to the DC area, Heather happily started in a new role in the major gifts office at the Kennedy Center for the Performing Arts, which included a nearly $20,000 salary bump from her last job. Although still technically working in a nonprofit, she now found herself in arts and entertainment, something Heather wouldn't have thought was possible just a few months prior.

Heather's newfound growth mindset stuck with her over the years in DC. She later joined me at Bossed Up Bootcamp when she started to feel she was hitting a plateau, and shortly thereafter she landed another new job (complete with better pay and benefits—again!), a communications-focused position for a small government contracting business.

"Ironically, taking all these risks and exploring different fields and positions was actually the most strategic thing I could have been doing," said Heather. "Now I have such a variety of experience, and I truly feel like I could rise to the occasion in any field I want to explore next."

Be Patient and Impatient

When I was four years old, I woke my dad up with a simple but dead-serious request: waffles, please! I have been a Leslie Knope–level waffle fanatic since I knew what they were called, and, while Mom was putting in a twelve-hour shift at the hospital that Saturday morning, my hankering for waffley goodness was my wake-up call (and consequently, my dad's too).

"You got it, Emmie," my dad yawned, as he arose from his slumber to mix me up a batch from scratch. We measured the flour together, and I watched him masterfully crack the eggs into the batter. I got to help stir it all together, and, before you know it, we poured that sweet-smelling magic into the waffle iron.

There was just one step we forgot: spraying on the oil.

My eyes were wide with anticipation when the timer finally went off and my dad pulled the waffle iron apart. But what we saw deflated us both: a caked-on mess that adhered like poured concrete to either side of the hot iron.

My dad, thoroughly discouraged, and no doubt feeling like he'd failed at the first thing he'd attempted to do for his little girl that morning, pulled the plug (figuratively and literally) and retreated in apology. His adult brain knew what a nightmare of a cleanup job awaited us. He figured the best way to proceed would be to dismantle the mess and soak it overnight. He didn't even want to look me in my little disappointed face, so he poured me a bowl of cereal and retreated back to bed to try his hand at a crossword puzzle.

Four-year-old me was not having this. Four-year-old me wanted some goddamn waffles. I didn't have the patience for waffles *tomorrow;* I wanted me some buttery, syrup-swimming waffles in my belly *now*. I also knew it wasn't nice to yell and scream at my dad, nor did that seem like an effective way to get what I wanted. Even I could tell how bummed out the poor guy was at trying and failing first thing in the morning.

So I grabbed a fork and pushed a kitchen chair from the table all the way to the counter. I hoisted myself up, sat on the counter-top, and got busy chiseling away at the crispy waffle amalgam. It was a daunting task. It wasn't a Belgian waffle iron; it was a cast iron one with those itty-bitty squares, but I wasn't worried about how long it would take. I was going to have some waffles. I got into the process, too. Whenever a sizeable chunk flew off, I popped it right in my mouth, a little appetizer to whet my palate.

I was up there for a while. It might have been an hour or so, and I was making an enormous mess. The powdered remains of burned waffle flew everywhere, coating most of my shirt and my hair. It was an arduous, monotonous task, but I had nowhere else to be. After what felt like forever, the iron looked decent enough for round two. It wasn't perfect, there were definitely portions of the iron that still had the baked-in remains of the failed first attempt, but it was mostly scraped clean. I wasn't allowed to use the waffle iron alone, so I burst into my dad's room to announce the good news. He was flabbergasted but pleasantly obliged my second request of the day. Before long we were chowing down on hot, syrupy waffles and cracking up over my dad's cheesy jokes.

Patience is a funny thing. My *impatience* has served me well over the years, because it means I start things. I don't settle for what's presented to me. When I think things can be better, I initiate new endeavors and set new goals. We need impatience to break through the inertia of life continuing on as it has always been. But once that impatience has you sweating over a new goal or effort, it doesn't stay feeling "new" for very long. We equally need patience to slog through the process of getting there. We need to call on our patience when the obstacles in our way seem too great, to sustain us through the process of learning through trial and error.

Patience has long been considered an important predictor of success.[5] The ability to delay gratification and balance your short-term desires and long-term ones is linked to a high number of successful outcomes. Kids who are more patient have more friends, get better grades, and score higher on standardized tests. The same thing could be said for adults, too. In fact, there are even several studies that link problems like addiction, smoking, and the inability to keep a job with low measures of patience and self-control.[6] Research shows that your patience is a better predictor of career and life success than your IQ.

We need to dance with patience *and* impatience with all our ambitions. They must peacefully and paradoxically exist within you at once. Call on your impatience when it's time to break out of "the way things are" and venture into new, audacious goal-setting territory, and then call on your patience when it's time to see your new vision through.

As Dweck's research on the growth mindset teaches us, even if you're naturally inclined to be more impatient than patient (or the other way around—a little *too* patient with life), you can always practice developing either of these qualities further.

Perfection Means Procrastination

My final words of warning as you set out on the journey to making that vision of yours a reality is to beware of the perfection trap. You know what I'm talking about. You want your next big move to be absolutely *stunning*. Let's say one of your goals is to start working as a freelance writer, so you pour your heart and soul into your first short story. You spend weeks, maybe even months, polishing it, plucking at it, until every single word is divine and you finally feel ready to share it with the world. You send it off to a dozen or so publications but hear nothing. Your confidence starts to wear. Maybe it's not as good as you thought it was, so you go back to the drawing board. You rework it for another few weeks and send it out again, this time to a whole other dozen or so publications. One bites! The editor wants to run it in next week's edition, but they have a handful of edits and comments for you, redlined throughout your "perfect" piece you've now spent three months of your life on.

You're devastated. How could the editor butcher your perfect piece like that? And how on earth could you be expected to make changes in such a short timeframe?

Don't let yourself get stuck in this kind of endless analysis paralysis. You don't know what opportunities you could be missing out on if you spend all your time on planning and such little time *getting to action*. Moving forward imperfectly almost always beats waiting for the perfect path forward.

Writer Liz Gilbert says that perfectionism is actually "just fear, in really good shoes."[7] And she's right. Wanting to be perfect and please everyone around us belies a deeper fear—a fear of not measuring up.

But we learn by dealing with difficulty. We grow by starting before we're 100 percent ready. You don't need to be confident that you're going to get it all right; you just need to be confident that you can figure it out as you go.

So hop to it, boss! Because *progress is in itself motivating*. Progress begets progress.

And as you set off on a new adventure, remember this: striving for sustainable success is a marathon, not a sprint. Focus on creating some forward momentum, and don't let a little failure on the road to success deter you.

In fact, in light of the inevitability of failure, let's practice some radical self-love instead: forgive yourself, right now, for the less-than-perfect decisions you will make. Know that you will learn from them. And proceed with the utmost confidence that, come hell or high water, you will figure it out.

Chapter 4

Speak It, Be It

So you're done playing the martyr, and you've started to take purposeful action to step up as the boss of your own life and career. There's just one little problem: that might not be how *other people* see you just yet.

In my years of working with women on overcoming internal roadblocks and navigating real-world barriers and biases, **assertive communication** remains the number one key skill that helps demonstrate your leadership capacity to those around you. Assertive communication is the bridge between knowing what you want out of your career and life and actually getting it. But here's the thing: assertiveness is riddled with tripwires and unique challenges for women in our world, and especially for women of color. Let's break it down.

Assertive Versus Aggressive

One of the biggest misconceptions that gets in the way is that the whole damn world seems to get "assertive" mixed up with "aggressive." Seriously. All the time. The two terms are used almost interchangeably in everyday conversation.

In reality, they differ in an important way: it all comes down to whose *rights* are being taken into consideration.

> **Being assertive means** being clear about your rights, wants, needs, and desires, *while considering* the rights, wants, needs, and desires of others.

> **Being aggressive means** being clear about your rights, wants, needs, and desires, *without regard for* the rights, wants, needs, and desires of others.

Being assertive is a two-way street, an open door, the start of a dialogue. Being aggressive is a one-way communiqué, a proclamation of rights, showing no interest in dialogue. Being assertive is an essential part of being a leader. Being aggressive is an essential part of being a bully. Both skills require using power on behalf of yourself, but only being *assertive* also includes using power on behalf of others.

Here's a simple metaphor to help remember the difference: imagine you're standing in a long line for Janelle Monae concert tickets to go on sale (as one should). For the sake of this example, let's pretend we live in a pre-StubHub world, mmmkay? So you've been waiting for hours along with some folks who even camped out all night to be first in line, but you're stuck somewhere in the middle. Five minutes before the tickets window opens, you see a person walk up to the front of the line and silently slip in among the all-nighters, looking fresh as a daisy and carrying a little quad of Starbucks lattes. You're steamed! Who the hell does she think she is?! You cross your arms, tap your toe, and point your eye-daggers right into the back of her head. All of a sudden, you hear a loud voice from behind you. Someone's standing out of line, calling the cutter out! "Excuse me!" she shouts. "The end of the line is back there," she says, pointing to the trail of people wrapped around the block. A hush falls over the crowd, some people start looking at the loud person behind you who's now carrying on and waving her arms in the air like she's lost her damn mind. "We've all been waiting here, you can't just swoop in front of all of us."

So who's being assertive and who's being aggressive in this scenario?

The question is tricky because being assertive is about substance, not style. So often the *style* with which we speak confuses the messages others receive (more on that in a minute), but being assertive or aggressive isn't a matter of style—it's a matter of content. Who is being respectful of the rights of everyone in this scenario? And who is just doing what's in her own best interest, regardless of anyone else?

Hopefully it's now more obvious that the silent but sneaky line cutter is the one being aggressive, as she's doing only what's in her own best interest—and perhaps the interest of a few of her friends. It's the person who dared to stand out and speak up who's being assertive, because she's standing up on behalf of herself and everyone else who's waiting. The cutter doesn't care who else wants tickets or how the whole queuing process works. But by speaking up, the person behind you is standing up for her own rights *and* upholding the rules of the game—the entire system and the other people in it.

Granted, the rules of the game for waiting in line are typically clearer than most situations we face at work. What are the rules of the game when it comes to handing out promotions? Pay raises?

Plum assignments? The same could be said about our personal relationships. What are the rules for divvying up the chores and childcare duties at home? Deciding on what to eat tonight or what to watch on Netflix? Determining who's going to whose relatives' homes for the holidays each year?

There are countless occasions when being comfortable with assertive communication can help you get what you want out of your career and life while also being considerate of others' interests in the matter. You can either approach these opportunities with a tolerance of the risk that's inherently involved in speaking your mind or try the strategy of staying pissed and sending eye-daggers across a crowd. I'm partial to the former, as I think it's a more effective use of my mental energy, personally.

Speaking of energy, being assertive isn't some skill you're born with or without, it's a choice—and a bold choice that requires some of your limited energy and effort. You couldn't possibly fight every battle and choose to be assertive in all situations, because you've got to reserve your energy for the times that matter most. I was recently on a 6 a.m. flight for a trip home to visit family. Early morning departures are no easy feat, but, fortunately, everyone on this flight knew the drill: flight attendants dim the cabin lights, barely anyone orders drinks, and we all agree to get some much-needed shut-eye. That is, everyone except for the two women sitting in the row behind me, one on either side of the aisle. They decided they'd much rather discuss the details of an upcoming bachelorette party they were planning for a friend, and, because they were seated across the aisle from each other, they figured shouting would be the best way to hold said discussion. Groan. I pulled down my sleep mask to peek, and literally no one else on the entire plane was talking. No one. Everyone else was asleep. And meanwhile you could probably hear the details of this conversation crystal clear through the airplane bathroom door. I wanted to turn around and say something, I really did. But words evaded me. I was so tired I tried to just drown them out and fall back asleep, but to no avail. I spent the entire two-hour ride feeling frustrated and paralyzed, and I kicked myself for weeks afterward for not saying anything. I teach people how to be assertive, for goodness' sake! Why couldn't I just turn around and ask for them to be a little more considerate of all the other passengers (myself included!) who were trying to get some shut-eye?

I've thought about that interaction often, because it hammers home the fact that being assertive isn't some characteristic you have or you don't. I have *way* less trouble being assertive when I have a tad more energy or when I've had my morning coffee. Being assertive requires resources—it takes energy, power, and thoughtfulness—that are easy to exhaust. You have to choose wisely when and how to draw on your limited resources when it matters most and know when you're running on empty.

If you've ever accidentally snapped at someone because *you* were overtired, stressed, or drained, then you're familiar with this already. Being conscious of others when speaking up for yourself requires thoughtful energy. That sometimes means taking a breath, considering your words carefully, and using your power to speak with strength, rather than staying silent for so long that, when you do finally speak up, you lash out in a flurry of pent-up anger and frustration. It's hard to be considerate of other people's rights, wants, and needs when you're exhausted from not standing up for your own.

How you choose to react to the many scenarios that call for an assertive response in the workplace matters a lot. After all, we know that perception can be powerful. Workplaces run by imperfect, biased humans are never a perfect meritocracy where everyone is judged based on performance alone. Your performance matters, sure, but how others *perceive* your performance is just as important.

One of my advisory board members, Lucy Gilson, especially knows this. As a professor and Management Department chair at the University of Connecticut's School of Business, one day she received a phone call from the dean of another business school who wanted her input on a hiring decision. He was looking to hire a senior tenured full professor, and the candidate was a colleague who Lucy had previously published with. The professor he was looking to hire had an amazing CV, had published extensively in peer-reviewed journals, was considered a leader in her field, an excellent teacher, and came highly recommended. What the dean wanted Lucy to talk to him about was how this colleague interacted with others, because during her on-campus interview, a couple of male faculty members had expressed some concerns that she could be a bit *aggressive.*

Lucy perked up. *Aggressive,* huh? She calmly asked the dean whether that's the word he intended to use, and she then walked him through a little vocabulary lesson. She explained the difference between assertive and aggressive and asked whether he thought she was actually steamrolling over others' rights like a bully, or whether she was just stating her case firmly while giving consideration to the needs of others—like a leader. Wasn't the university, after all, looking to hire a very senior faculty member who they would want to have opinions and thoughts grounded in research and expertise?

There was silence on the other end of the line.

With each passing moment, Lucy started to worry that perhaps she'd overstepped her bounds. Maybe *she* had been too assertive with her unsolicited linguistics lesson—yikes! But when he finally did break the silence, the dean said, "Hey, can you say that again? I'm writing this down. I've never heard it put that way before."

It's true. This distinction *is* rarely articulated, but it's important. By calling attention to the difference between "assertive" and "aggressive," Lucy helped the dean shed the negative connotation that comes when a woman is assertive and her views and opinions are all too often mislabeled as aggressive. Lucy's colleague got the job, and this dean continues to share this story with others to this day. Being assertive and daring to make your voice heard always comes with the risk of being misunderstood, but those risks are outweighed by the potential rewards.

SPOTLIGHT

"Just do it, you are worth it."

Liz was ready for a new job. She'd been working in emergency response management for six years and was craving more work-life balance and a change of pace. After four interviews with a conference production company, she was confident she had the position in the bag, but she also knew switching industries would involve taking a pay cut. She'd been making nearly six figures in emergency management, whereas the position she'd been interviewing for was listed at $50,000. That said,

Liz was prepared to meet them halfway in exchange for all the perks that came with the new industry: more predictable work hours, being part of a strong team, and seeing a whole different side of the working world. So as the conversation turned to money, Liz didn't hesitate.

"My line in the sand was $75K," Liz told me. "And I felt it was fair given the very transferable skills I had. So I just told them I simply cannot walk away from the job that I have for any less."

She acknowledges the privileged, powerful position she found herself in at the time: Liz had a steady job that paid the bills (even if it wasn't a job she loved), and she wasn't going to be heartbroken if this offer didn't pan out. She wasn't desperately fleeing a bad situation, but, rather, wanted to ensure her next job would set her up for sustainable success.

Her prospective employer was willing to play ball, and offered her a $65,000 starting salary with quarterly bonuses that would total $75K a year. Sure, the bonus structure came with some tax differences, but Liz appreciated their willingness to find an amicable solution. Plus, they offered an additional sales commission on top of it all and reassured her she would be well taken care of financially.

"I'm very proud of that moment," Liz said, reflecting on how she asked for $25,000 more than the starting offer without hesitation. "I was totally committed to it, so I just confidently blurted it out. I was almost surprised at how I got the words out without hesitation, because, at the end of the day, I felt I had nothing to lose."

Liz signed all the paperwork reflecting her final negotiated offer and was off to the races on this exciting new chapter of her career. But two quarters into working for the new company,

Liz realized there was something wrong: her bonus wasn't present in her paycheck. She talked to the team accountant, who knew nothing about the matter, so instead brought the issue up with their CEO, who suggested they chat over coffee.

He acknowledged the issue and agreed that something had to be done. He suggested they make an adjustment to "make her whole" at the close of the next quarter, and Liz begrudgingly agreed.

"Apparently the direction was never communicated to payroll," said Liz, "and by speaking up about it, I was made to feel like *I* was making a fuss, when all I was asking for was for them to follow through on what they'd agreed to in my contract."

But, by the time the end of her first year came around, things still weren't adding up, and at this point Liz was beyond frustrated. She not only had asserted herself in the initial negotiation, but now she felt like she had to fight tooth and nail to get paid, too.

"At the end of the year, I had only been paid $63,000 of the $75,000 I'd been promised," Liz told me, "even when accounting for tax withholdings. Just imagine if I hadn't been willing to stick up for my worth again and again and again? No one would have caught the error on their side of things and then my initial negotiation would have been for nothing."

After the better part of a year of being placated, it became clear to Liz that a solution was there, but no one was putting in the effort to make it happen. Irate with the way this organization conducted its business and treated staff, Liz started exploring her options elsewhere.

"It felt like I'd been tricked into the job under false pretenses," said Liz. "I was owed money, the CEO had validated that I was owed money, and nothing had been done. Frankly, I'm just not going to work for people who conduct themselves like that."

Just after her one-year anniversary there, Liz left in an ironic twist to return to her former employer in a totally different role. She returned to the world of emergency management but in a training capacity, where she's been happily employed for years since then.

But, on her way out, she wrote an email that included all the details on what she was owed and advocated once again for her to be made whole. The firm finally complied and sent her a hefty check to reconcile the error, but, throughout it all, Liz was made to feel as though she was some kind of troublemaker.

"I was just trying to get what they'd already agreed to," Liz told me, "and daring to speak up because this was wrong and needed to be rectified."

In thinking back on her tumultuous year, Liz acknowledge that it would have been all too easy to just let things slide and not speak up. "I think that we all believe there's a 'nice' way to go about this and that because people aren't purposefully being 'mean' we shouldn't speak up about it," she said. "But that's ridiculous. There's no reason to just let things slide when they happen to you. You don't have to be 'rude' to ask for what you need, and there's no reason to be so afraid of doing it."

Liz asserted herself, again and again. She spoke up about what she was owed, advocating for herself in a way that was professional but persistent. Ultimately, her colleagues responded appropriately, if a bit late. But if your colleagues don't? Well, Liz said, "that's something you need to know about your workplace if you're going to be investing your time there."

That year gave Liz the confidence to move forward in her career with a "just do it" attitude when it comes to speaking up and making her voice heard. "The consequences that we think are there aren't usually on the table," says Liz. "It's rare that companies just up and fire you. But we seem to think our jobs are *always* on the line, which keeps far too many of us silent, for far too long."

At the end of the day, only you can weigh the risks and opportunities that come with being assertive. But if Liz learned one thing from her experience, it's that no one else is going to stick up for you, so you'd better be ready to stick up for yourself. "Just do it," she said, "because you are so worth it."

Tap Dancing on a Tightrope

But here's the rub: even though being assertive is an essential skill for making things happen as a leader, it isn't always appreciated when it comes *from a woman*. It can feel like tap dancing on a tightrope: you want to come across as strong and earn people's respect, but you don't want to offend or overstep your bounds. You want to be serious but sweet. You want to be authoritative but democratic. You want to show that you can handle things but also want to show that you're a good team player. It feels like, no matter what you say or how you say it, you're always at risk of saying the wrong thing.

Nicki Minaj broke down this challenging binary in an unaired clip from her *E! True Hollywood Story* documentary that made its way to YouTube:

> When you're a girl, you have to be, like, everything. You have
> to be dope at what you do, but you have to be super sweet, and
> you have to be sexy, and you have to be this, and you have to
> be that, and you have to be nice. . . . I can't be all those things
> at once. I'm a human being. When I am assertive, I'm a bitch.
> When a man is assertive, he's a boss. He's bossed up. No nega-
> tive connotation behind "bossed up," but lots of negative conno-
> tation behind "being a bitch."[1]

Sadly, she was critiqued for these statements, which some
called a "rant," and ended up removing the footage before the final
airing of the documentary. She even ended the clip herself by saying, "Don't use this footage, please, it's just gonna make me look
stupid." The way all this went down basically proved her point:
people don't like assertive women.

An enormous body of research has found evidence of this troubling perception problem, too. Women who are seen being assertive
are deemed less likeable, and often even less *capable,* to a greater
extent than men expressing the same assertiveness.[2] This inverse
correlation between assertiveness and likeability for women is
sadly just as likely to appear among men judging assertive women
as it is when women are asked to judge women. In other words,
both women *and* men judge assertive women more harshly.

That's partly why speaking up can feel like such a risk, and
many women opt to stay silent, so as to avoid the very real possibility of backlash. In a *New York Times* op-ed called "Speaking
While Female," Sheryl Sandberg and Adam Grant dove deep into
the data behind "why women stay quiet at work." Study after study
showed that when men speak up more and contribute ideas that

bring in new revenue, they're seen as more helpful and get significantly higher performance evaluations. But when women do the same, it does improve their managers' perception of their performance or helpfulness at all.[3]

But wait—isn't being assertive part of being a good leader? The answer is yes—and that's why this is such a catch-22. As we already discussed, the first step in building your boss identity is to take purposeful action. That often means asserting yourself—putting out there what you want and then taking the lead on making it happen. But although being a leader (of yourself and of others) requires being assertive, that behavior runs contrary to age-old gender stereotypes of what makes for a "good woman."

Still too many of us are taught that "good girls" are nice, caring, sweet, quiet, coy, unintrusive, pretty, smiling, and either virginal or vixen-like, depending on the sexual appetite of the person you ask. These messages are rarely overt—but instead permeate our media, the way we praise girls and women, and the everyday unconscious assumptions we all make about women and men.

As Shirley Chisholm, the first African American congresswoman, famously said, "The emotional, sexual, and psychological stereotyping of females begins when the doctor says, 'It's a girl.'"

This double bind wouldn't be such a big deal if our world operated like a perfect meritocracy. If we were evaluated, promoted, and awarded based on achievements alone, I'm convinced we'd live a much more gender-equitable world. But likeability counts and perception is powerful.

So what's a boss to do? How can you ensure that you're being heard and taken seriously, without coming off as a bitch (at least not *all* the time)?

1. Pick Your Battles

Being assertive isn't the "right" way to communicate, it's simply *one* strategy to further your goals. So consider your audience, and choose mindfully when you want to go to the mat on the issues you feel strongly about. Being assertive is a tool I want in your toolbox, but at the end of the day, it's always *your choice* when to use it.

Remember, being assertive and standing your ground takes energy, so you decide when to make the effort, and when to let it slide. Research from Stanford shows that women who are selectively assertive—meaning they know when to boss up and when to go with the flow—are more likely to be seen as having that elusive "executive presence" and, in turn, are more likely to be promoted.[4] Consider your goals and know your audience, and choose strategically when to speak up for your rights, wants, and needs.

2. Intent, Then Content

When you *are* choosing to be assertive, here's a great little trick that behavioral psychologists recommend to counter some of that unconscious bias BS.[5] Normally, when we speak our mind, we say our piece and *then* we explain it further.

For instance, you might say:

"Hey—can you turn down your radio? I'm trying to work and I can't focus with your music blasting into my workspace."

Researchers found that both men *and* women can reduce negative perceptions that come with being assertive by just reversing the order: lead with your intent, then your assertive content.

The reversed version would sound like this:

"Hey—I'm trying to work and I can't focus with your music blasting into my workspace. Can you turn down your radio?"

Read them aloud. Can you hear the difference? It's amazing how such a simple switch seems to change the tone. When you give people a little context as to *why* you're about to be assertive, before you say your assertive bit, they're much more likely to see where you're coming from.

3. Purpose over Perception

Here's the reality: you actually *can't* perfectly control how others perceive you. You can't! Even Beyoncé and Taylor Swift, who have entire teams of people employed full time to help control their image, don't always get it right. So for us mere mortals? Let's get used to the fact that someone might be judging us unfairly when we speak our mind, and then let's get back to work anyway.

As my favorite researchers in the *Harvard Business Review* say:

> The time and energy spent on managing these perceptions can ultimately be self-defeating. Overinvestment in one's image diminishes the emotional and motivational resources available for larger purposes. People who focus on how others perceive them are less clear about their goals, less open to learning from failure, and less capable of self-regulation.[6]

You can't spend your limited time and energy trying to get everyone to like you when you're on the path to making your vision a reality. After all, when you're daring to do you, there's always someone calling you a bitch behind your back. Hell, maybe you'll join me in co-opting the word and take it back to describe a woman who's unafraid of being the boss—*a bad bitch*. After all, as Tina Fey so perfectly pointed out, "Bitches get stuff done."

That said, of course not everyone can afford to take the risks of speaking out and making their voice heard, only to be sidelined and ostracized in their workplace or, God forbid, lose their job. The more we have to lose, the more risk averse we become, and understandably so.

That's why all this advice on what you can do (and, really, this entire book) needs to be coupled with broader, systemic solutions. As Grant and Sandberg go on to detail in their op-ed, organizations need to find structural ways to disrupt unconscious bias, like using a gender-blind screening process for resumes at the start of the hiring process. Further, leaders of all genders need to make it easier for women to speak up, by being explicit about encouraging input from everyone and calling out interruptions, which disproportionately silence women.[7]

Another thing we can all do better? Stick up for the assertive boss women among us. If a woman in your office makes her voice heard, only to be called "aggressive" or asked to "calm down," don't just be a bystander—be an advocate for her! It might be as simple as saying, "No, I think she's on to something . . ." or "I agree with her" to keep the conversation going.

Top-level women in the Obama White House popularized a similar strategy—called **amplification**—when a 2016 *Washington Post* article about it went viral.[8] When a man would restate an idea raised earlier in conversation by a woman, other women in the room would restate the point—and give proper credit. It's hard to stick up for yourself over and over again, so let's get in the habit of sticking up for others when they need it. You can even ask for verbal backup when you've got something tough to say and want to do everything you can to ensure your message is heard.

Men can and must do this, too. When women are called "aggressive," it's another way of telling us we're out of line and violating gender norms. It's a not-so-subtle way of telling a woman that she's not being nice, as though we're supposed to be nice all the time, to everyone. Men can amplify women's voices, too, and we should feel free to ask them to.

The ultimate solution? More boss women. It's true. "As more women enter the upper echelons of organizations," Sandberg and Grant write, "people become more accustomed to women's contributing and leading." More boss women makes being "a bossy woman" less of a thing. So, to make this kind of culture change a reality, we need pioneers to push the envelope and grow their power, so that powerful, outspoken women become, well, nothing notable.[9]

SPOTLIGHT

"Setting boundaries with my mother made it easier to do with my clients."

Loryn is a thirty-four-year-old independent consultant who works as a digital strategist on behalf of nonprofits, progressive advocacy organizations, and small businesses. She and her husband are working to achieve specific financial goals before they feel comfortable starting a family. Like most Americans, they're worried about the high cost of having a child and want to make that decision prudently.

Loryn's mother, however, wants to know when she can expect a grandchild.

"It came up again on a phone call with her recently," Loryn told me, "and I thought about how my therapist and I have been working on having me draw more healthy boundaries in my life—this seemed like the perfect opportunity."

As a black woman working in a predominantly white, male-dominated field, Loryn knows how hard it is to speak up, say no, and draw those kinds of boundaries.

"I've had a hard time being assertive at work, especially with people in some kind of position of power over me," said Loryn. "When you're someone on the margins—a person of color, woman, young, or all the above like me—there's a very real fear that the penalties for speaking out will be more severe."

And, when it comes to family especially, there's the guilt of letting someone you love *down* when you dare to put boundaries up. For Loryn, who's always had a bit of a tenuous relationship with her more-than-a-tad-controlling mother, that guilt is real.

"I'll always be this fourteen-year-old girl she's trying to raise to be a lady," Loryn confessed with a laugh. "She just wants me to be a woman with *her* rules, on *her* terms."

Part of the challenge is that Loryn's life looks much different than her mother's ever has. Loryn is one of three children who were raised by her young mother full time. As a millennial working woman, she's part of a generation with more student debt than our parents have ever dealt with, on top of sharply rising housing prices that produce a stark contrast to the realities of starting a family a generation ago.

"Since being laid off from my last job," Loryn shared, "I

decided to hang my own shingle and pursue freelancing instead. While it's going very well, that also means some of the things that would make having a baby just aren't in place, like health care, a predictable income, or any kind of parental leave."

So, when Loryn's mother brought up the subject of having babies—*again*—on the phone, Loryn decided to be assertive about her boundaries, so that she and her mom could maintain a healthy relationship without the undue stress of all this baby pressure.

"It's on the to-do list," replied Loryn. "But as I told you before, having kids is expensive, and this question really strikes a chord with me because Neal and I are not in the financial place we want to be to make that decision just yet."

"I just need to know when you'll be thinking about doing that," her mom replied.

"I promise you'll be the first to know," said Loryn. "It's our decision and it'll happen on our time. So I really need you to not ask me about this again."

Her mom replied with the standard rhetoric women of a certain age start to hear. "Well, no one is ever really *ready* to have a child," she argued. But Loryn stood firm.

Loryn felt a huge surge of control over the situation afterward. "I told her, I put it out on the table that I don't appreciate that question, and now there's a line in the sand," said Loryn. "If she crosses it—which I hope she doesn't—I'll just have to reduce contact with her for a while, which might be what our relationship needs."

Like all of us, Loryn feels an understandable sense of obligation to her mother, and sometimes the guilt over drawing those boundaries is intense. "But I want to be able to talk to her about anything without feeling like she's going to put all her expectations on me," said Loryn. "When the guilt hits and I feel like I'm a bad daughter, I recognize that I love my mom, but I don't have to want to talk to her all the time. It's a hard pill to swallow because of what we're taught about mothers and daughters, but I ask myself, 'Is this boundary going to help me maintain my sanity and maintain my relationship with her over the long run?' And the answer is yes, even if it will frustrate her in the short term."

Loryn and her husband will be making the decision on when to start their family together as a couple when they're ready. By standing up for her own boundaries, Loryn's also standing up for the life she wants to provide for her child someday. By advocating for herself and her future child in this domain, Loryn has found being assertive easier in other aspects of her life.

"Once I got comfortable setting boundaries with my mother," Loryn added, "it made setting boundaries with my clients easier. It made me feel empowered to be honest about what I need, honest about what I can provide, and honest when I *can't* provide something."

Recently, Loryn's client load was so intense she had to tell a friend who had paid her a deposit up front for her services that she actually didn't have the bandwidth to come through for her at that time. Loryn issued her a refund right away, and her friend was understanding and even expressed interest in working together in the future when Loryn *did* have the capacity.

"I thought to myself, if I can tell my mother, 'no, I don't want to talk about having babies right now,' it actually made it easier to set other boundaries in my life, too."

Dear White People...

Any woman navigating the leadership-likeability balancing act might feel like she's tap dancing on a tightrope. But, for women of color, it's like adding a juggling routine on top of it all.

Although I certainly have Latina blood, I present white and have plenty of white privilege working for me. That means I've lived my life quietly benefitting from a whole slew of privileges I was blissfully unaware of until relatively recently. No one ever called me angry or felt physically threatened by my assertiveness, a response familiar to many women who have to contend with the "angry black woman" trope. I've never been dismissed as being spicy or feisty, as so many Latina women are. And no one remarked at how surprised they were that I wasn't shy, soft-spoken, or submissive, like so many Asian women hear all the damn time.

The reality is, being assertive is challenging for all women, but it's especially challenging for women of color. This is something that we need to talk honestly about (especially us white and white-ish folks) if we're going to make significant, inclusive progress.

Catalyst, a nonprofit research organization, calls the barriers faced by women of color at the workplace the "concrete ceiling." "The metaphor of a 'concrete ceiling' stands in sharp contrast to that of the 'glass ceiling,'" says Catalyst president Sheila Wellington. "Not only is the 'concrete ceiling' reported to be more difficult to penetrate, women of color say they cannot see through it to glimpse the corner office."[10] Ascending to the highest echelons of power and leadership is hard for any woman, but for women of color who live in a world where even seeing role models who share your skin color is rare, it's hard to even *imagine* for yourself.

Let's remember that unconscious bias based on gender doesn't exist in a vacuum. Gender bias is constantly intersecting with bias based on a whole array of factors—things like race, gender identity, sexual orientation, ability, age, class, you name it. The list is always growing. The troubling reality is that we humans have been drawing lines between "us" and "them" since the dawn of time. It's what we do. It's ingrained in our psychology.

But we can rise above our own wiring by first acknowledging that we're all a little biased. There doesn't need to be some room full of white men huddled around some grand Patriarchy Plan plotting against women and people of color (although nowadays that feels more and more plausible) for systemic racism, sexism, ageism, and more kinds of bias to persist. These biases can be covert—many of us don't even realize the assumptions and stereotypes we carry with us into our everyday interactions. And that means that there's no malintent required to perpetuate injustice. We're all guilty. But we're not hopeless.

That's why it's critical that we acknowledge the various intersecting levels of bias each of us faces and help call it out—just like Lucy did on that phone call with her department chair. It might be as simple as asking, "What do you mean?" when someone labels a colleague as "aggressive," "angry," "feisty," or much worse. Language matters, and, when we let those labels slide, we miss a teachable moment for everyone.

And hey, fellow white people: calling that kind of behavior out is *not* the sole responsibility of people of color. Can you imagine how exhausting it would be for a black woman to try to correct every single unintentionally ignorant person that she encounters? I can't! It's annoying enough dealing with everyday sexism in this world! So come on, white ladies, let's put our privilege to work on this. Be a vocal ally—and, yes, let's ask our male colleagues to be vocal allies, too.

We all know how hard it is to speak up for yourself when *you're* the one being mistreated (hell, that's what this entire chapter is about!), so let's do each other a favor and help lift the burden from the shoulders of those who are under fire most often, shall we? Let's be there for each other in a time of need. That's what real bossed up women do—we lift each other up even as we're still fighting for ourselves.

As we talk further about honing your own assertive communication through this intersectional lens, I want to talk about code switching. Code switching is a practice familiar to those in first-generation families and many communities of color.

It's defined by linguists as the practice of alternating between two or more languages or varieties of language in conversation.

For many in communities of color, the way you speak with friends of your same community group might differ drastically from the way you speak in a boardroom.

No one exemplified this better than Keegan-Michael Key and Jordan Peele in their hilarious thirty-second sketch called "Phone Call." The two men are speaking on their respective cell phones, as they approach one another at the corner of a sidewalk. Peele's character is waiting for the light to turn so he can cross the street. Key's character is speaking to his wife about buying theater tickets for her birthday. As the men approach, they give a quick nod to acknowledge one another, and their speech starts to sound more like a Jay-Z album full of low, super-masculine undertones. The men code-switch into African American Vernacular English, or AAVE, which was once called *ebonics*—a term that is no longer considered particularly politically correct. (Ya hear that, white folks?) Key suddenly starts referencing "thee-ate-er" tickets and says to his wife, "I'll pick yo' ass up around six." As the men part ways, Peele's character takes on an effeminate tone as he grips the phone and exclaims, "Oh my god, Christian, I totally just almost got mugged." As usual, Key and Peele bring hilarity to a topic that is *so* real for so many people of color navigating everyday life. I highly recommend checking out the skit for yourself on Comedy Central's website for the full effect.[11]

Although no one should *have* to adjust their natural way of talking, I'm a big believer in the pragmatism behind the practice. There's no shame in that game. Some would say you're being inauthentic when you code-switch, but I'm calling bullshit. It's a strategic move! The basis of all effective communication boils down to keeping your speech goal oriented (know what you're trying to achieve) and audience centered (consider how your audience is going to best receive your message). Code switching is a simple change in tactic by which you smartly adjust your approach based on what works for your audience. This is a good example of a communication practice that stems from minority communities that all people can learn from.

Granted, feeling like you *have* to mask who you are at work is exhausting. It pulls from your limited mental faculties and distracts you from focusing on your purpose. The privilege of feeling free to be your authentic self at work is something many white men and, to an extent, white women often take for granted. But there's a clear difference between feeling like you have to mask yourself and strategically choosing to switch up your style and delivery based on your goals and audience. Although I'm not a proponent of environments that perpetuate the former, I don't judge anyone who chooses to employ the latter.

So let's break down more research-backed strategies for aligning your visual, vocal, and verbal communication when you're strategically choosing to be seen as more assertive. But first I want to emphasize that this is not intended as any kind of policing of women's speech. As I said earlier, this is not the only or the right way to communicate. Being assertive is merely *one strategy* that can bolster your boss identity and help others see you as the leader you are. It's a tool I want every woman to have in her toolbox and feel comfortable using but that by no means is the tool you use for every job or in every conversation. When you *do* want to come across as assertive, a big part of getting your message across has to do with style.

Tricks of the Trade

When choosing to make your voice heard assertively—at work or elsewhere—there are plenty of stylistic techniques to ensure you're setting yourself up for the best outcomes. First, let's remember that it's substance that counts when determining whether someone's being assertive or aggressive, so these strategies are just the cherry on top. And, second, remember that being assertive is always your choice. But when you *are* choosing to make that assertive move, these tricks of the trade can help you effectively get your message across.

We'll break these strategies down in terms of verbal (the words you use), vocal (how you sound while speaking), and visual (how you look while speaking) best practices.

Verbal
Buzzwords, Bye!
We all have them—they're those tiny, meaningless utterances that permeate our speech without us even knowing they're there. "Um,"

"er," "uh," "like," and "you know" are some of the most common ones I encounter. Mindlessly adding "right?" at the end of most of my sentences is a personal habit I'm still working on curbing, too.

Much of the reason our everyday speech is riddled with buzz-words stems from our discomfort with silence. When you're asked a question, for example, you might be quick to start answering before you've given yourself time to think, thus falling back on buzzwords for their instantaneous, if meaningless, ability to fill the void. When you're midway through expressing yourself but need to collect your thoughts, you might use buzzwords to buy time to choose your next words carefully. Often, buzzwords pepper our speech right at the moments when we're being most thoughtful and pensive—when we're thinking of what we want to say next.

But, unfortunately, they don't make you *seem* very thoughtful to those listening to you. Buzzwords detract from your message because they distract auditorily, often making you come off as ner-vous or uncomfortable.

Silence, as it turns out, is a powerful tool for making an asser-tive impression. Instead of falling back on buzzwords, allow your-self to pause, think, and then speak. With silence, you'll be seen as thoughtful, not slow. I promise, it only feels like a long, awkward pause to you. Feel free to take your time.

At their best, buzzwords can make you look nervous or flus-tered, and, at their worst, they can completely misrepresent your message. Back in 2008, Senate hopeful Caroline Kennedy used the buzzwords "you know" so pervasively in a televised interview (142 times in a five-minute clip) that even though it was a meaningless buzzword, it changed the entire tone of her message, causing her to come off as patronizing and dismissive, despite the very differ-ent substance of what she was saying.[12]

It sounds like it should be easy, but reprogramming your buzzword-loving brain can be a challenge. First, identify which buzzwords you unconsciously rely on. Record yourself speaking into the camera on your smartphone or computer and practice giving a presentation, interview responses, or speech as though you were really up there speaking it. Then play it back and see what buzzwords jump out. If you're having trouble identifying your buzzwords on your own, ask a trusted colleague, friend, or loved one to help point out any buzzwords you use, especially when you're nervous, such as in the middle of an actual presentation.

Once you identify those filler words, work on actively replacing them with a pause or breath. Using a mock scenario again, bring in a friend or partner who will give you a visual cue every time you accidentally make the slip. A former professor of mine tended to fall back on buzzwords when at cocktail parties and had her husband squeeze her hand or arm gently to give her the silent signal. Practice eliminating your buzzwords in low-risk scenarios first, such as placing your order when eating out, and that practice will help you be ready to replace buzzwords with powerful pauses when it matters most.

Quit the Qualifiers

Another habit that detracts from our assertiveness? Qualifying our speech. Speech qualifiers are the little preambles that can sneak in before what you're about to say and discredit you in the process. You might *want* to say:

"I don't agree with that assessment at all."

But with a qualifier before it, it might come out like this:

"This is just my opinion, but I don't agree with that assessment at all."

Don't cut yourself off at the knees before you even take a step, boss! Watch out for these common qualifiers, which serve no purpose other than to detract from the validity of what you're about to say:

"This might be irrelevant/unrelated, but . . ."

"I'm sorry, but . . ."

"I'm just thinking out loud here, but . . ."

"I might just be being crazy, but . . ."

When you're purposefully trying to come off as assertive, these qualifiers have got to go. If you're worried about coming across as too harsh or abrasive, instead of detracting from your own credibility with qualifiers, opt for that aforementioned "intent, then content" strategy I detailed earlier. For example you might say:

"I want to ensure we're considering all options here, because I don't agree with that assessment at all."

Sharing your intent is different from qualifying your speech. Intent explains your "why," but qualifiers just discredit what you're about to say.

Of course when you're *actually* uncertain and not in a situation in which you feel the need to respond assertively, qualifiers might be helpful. For instance if you're asked the time and you genuinely aren't sure, feel free to qualify your response! There's not much to lose by not coming across as assertive in that situation. But, when you're looking to boost your assertiveness, qualifiers will not help your cause.

No Means No

There's a saying that "No" is a complete sentence. It's probably *the most* assertive sentence. In October 2015, Hillary Clinton was asked by debate moderator Anderson Cooper whether she wanted to respond to a somewhat incoherent critique levied against her by primary contestant Senator Lincoln Chafee of Rhode Island. She looked right at Anderson, smiled, and said, "No." It was a brazen, confident move that made headlines the next day. When you're looking to give a strong impression, it doesn't get more powerful than a single "no."

Of course, saying no is rarely that easy. We want to apologize, explain ourselves, and be agreeable. We're afraid of disappointing people or being seen as unkind. All that is totally fair, but it's not assertive. I realize that saying no isn't easy, but it's tremendously impactful—hell, it's the entire subject of my TEDx talk, "The Power of No." If you're really looking to up your assertiveness and come across as powerfully and forcefully as you can, don't overexplain, and don't sugarcoat it when "no" is your final answer.

Instead of declining a request like this:

"Ah! I'm so sorry, I wish I could be there but I have a doctor's appointment and I really can't move it again. . . . I feel terrible but I'm so happy you're launching this new initiative!"

A more assertive response might sound like this:

"I'm afraid I'm not available then. Let me know if I can support another way—congrats!"

Being comfortable with "no" takes time—and it takes real power. Think about your audience—the way you say no to your friend's request for drinks will sound different from how you get yourself out of an assignment your boss just asked you to take on.

But, in our burnout culture, *you* draw the boundaries. And, yes, sometimes that means saying no. There couldn't be a more important skill to practice to help craft the career and life you want. If we don't, our very ability to direct our lives may slip through our fingers.

Poet Iain Thomas said it best:

And every day, the world will drag you by the hand, yelling, "This is important! And this is important! You need to worry about this! And this! And this!"

And each day, it's up to you to yank your hand back, put it on your heart and say, "No. This is what's important."[13]

Saying no makes room for more "oh hell yes!" in your life. In fact, one way to get more comfortable saying no is to focus on what you're actually saying yes to when you have to say it. When you tell your boss no because the deadline is when you're scheduled to be out of office, you're actually saying yes to being fully present at your brother's wedding or your precious vacation. When you say no to attending 6 a.m. yoga, you're giving yourself permission to say yes to eight hours of sleep and subsequently to being fully functional for the entirety of the day ahead of you.

It's worth the effort to practice saying no when the stakes are relatively low to get comfortable with causing a little discomfort, if that's what it takes to assert yourself. After all, if you don't actively, assertively create the boundaries you need to craft the career and life you want, no one else will do it for you.

Vocal

Another way our style can impact the substance of our message is through our vocal tone. Unfortunately, not all vocal tones are heard equally in our world—and, of course, there's a gendered component to it.

The policing of women's voices goes all the way back to the Roman Empire and the first recorded critique of an unusually assertive woman—one who insisted upon speaking on her own behalf in the Roman court. She was described as having an "unnatural yapping" and a "bark." Margaret Thatcher's own biographer once noted how, after working with a speech coach, "the hectoring tones of the housewife gave way to softer notes," which he considered a political win. And of course, decades later in 2016 we saw Hillary Clinton's voice labeled "shrill," "bitter," "grating," and compared to a "nagging wife."

As a podcaster, I'm familiar with people who've got a thing or two to say about my voice. Many of my fellow podcasters get hate online from listeners who feel they're doing you a favor by telling you how to adjust your natural speaking tone to be less annoying to their ears. Female journalists on NPR, for instance, have been critiqued for sounding too juvenile, "like high-school girls." Ira Glass covered the phenomenon on an episode of *This American Life* and was surprised by the intensity of the complaints NPR receives about its female producer's vocal tones. "They call these women's voices 'unbearable,'" says Ira, quoting a long list of listener hate-mail excerpts: "Excruciating, annoyingly adolescent, beyond annoying, difficult to pay attention, so severe as to cause discomfort, can't stand the pain, distractingly disgusting, could not get over how annoyed I was, I am so appalled, detracts from the credibility of the journalist, degrades the value of the reportage, it's a choice, very unprofessional."[14]

Glass goes on to mention this interesting fact: the show had never received a letter about his voice, which shares many of the characteristics that earned his female coworkers so many complaints. And this NPR example was just looking at vocal tone feedback on the male/female binary! For trans women and men, vocally "passing" is a huge part of establishing a broader gender identity. However you slice it, vocal tone plays a major role in how we are perceived.

What all these critiques boil down to is that in many ways feminine-sounding voices are seen as less authoritative and trustworthy. This goes right back to unconscious gender bias: whether the critics are aware of it or not, these assumptions have everything to do with how we traditionally think about who *should be* leaders and who has historically been in positions of power: the guys! When women's voices sound too divergent from the stereotypical male voices of power, there's a cognitive disconnect.

It goes without saying that this just isn't right. It's another one of those frustrating double binds that women on the rise run into all the damn time. We shouldn't *have* to sound like men to be taken seriously. Being and sounding like a woman doesn't detract from our competence or authority, so why should we have to manipulate our voices as such?

Well, right or wrong, research on two vocal habits in particular makes a compelling case for adjusting your style when it furthers your goals. As I always say, you shouldn't overinvest in modulating your style to placate the haters—it's an endless endeavor! But bringing awareness to unconscious habits that might be getting in the way of making the impression you want can be empowering. Choose to affect your style when it matters most to you. There is no *wrong* way to sound, but when you're trying to come off as assertive, these are the two vocal habits to avoid:

Vocal Fry

You know the way a Kardashian speaks? Just imagine Kim Kardashian saying "OMG, *yaaaaas,*" for a moment. Are you imagining a low, creaky tone? That's vocal fry.

It's a low glottalization produced by a fluttering of the vocal cords that some doctors actually call vocal abuse. Although this sound is commonly found among young American women, many men are all about the fry, too. I've never been more aware of vocal fry than when I provide trainings or speak at conferences on college campuses. For whatever reason, the campus environment seems to be a breeding ground for this vocal trend, where two-thirds of women have been found to fry.[15]

In a large national sample of Americans, researchers at Duke University found that vocal fry "is interpreted negatively," leaving the speaker "perceived as less competent, less educated, less trustworthy, less attractive, and less hirable."[16] Although smaller, earlier studies found that vocal fry was appreciated by millennial women (who associated its usage with "upwardly mobile," "urban-oriented" young women), the Duke study found vocal fry made a negative impression on everyone, regardless of age, and most irritated women over forty. The negative judgments were found to be stronger for women's voices than for men's (surprise, surprise), and the researchers concluded that women should avoid the fry to "maximize labor market opportunities." On a *CBS Sunday Morning* episode covering the topic, Faith Salie shared that vocal fry left young women sounding "disengaged" and "uninterested," which is certainly not the impression you'd want to give during a presentation, interview, or speech.[17]

If you find yourself unintentionally frying your way through your everyday conversations, there are a few ways to adjust your tone—whenever your particular goals and audience might inspire you to do so:

Try it!

First, practice some deep-breathing exercises. Breathe in all the way until you feel your belly expand and lungs fill up. Then, slowly exhale all the air out. Put your hand on your belly to ensure your body is expanding as you inhale. Repeat this three times in a row at the start and end of your workday. Not only will it help your body get in the habit of taking in more air, but it's also a great way to reduce stress instantaneously.

Part of the underlying cause of vocal fry is a lack of air movement through the vocal cords during speech. Breathing exercises like this, especially in advance of a big speech or interview, can help you ditch the fry.

If deep breathing doesn't help, try raising your pitch ever so slightly. You don't need to go all *Pitch Perfect* aca-awesome with it, just a slight increase in the notes you're hitting will make a huge difference and bring your speech out of the gravelly verbal gutter.

Finally, pay careful attention to your enunciation at the *end* of phrases and sentences. Because vocal fry stems from a lack of oxygen, we tend to trail off instead of pronouncing everything through to the end. If you focus on articulating the entire sentence through, you'll fuel your speech with more oxygen and reduce the vocal fry effect.

Speak Up, but Without Upspeak?

It seems that upspeak was the 1980s equivalent of what vocal fry is now: a linguistic innovation led by young women and yet widely disparaged by everyone else.

Upspeak is shorthand for the lilting intonation of speaking that leads the user to sound like every phrase or sentence contains a question. It involves ending your sentences at a consistently higher pitch than where you start them. Think of Cher in the 1990s hit *Clueless* (brilliantly portrayed by the great Alicia Silverstone). She was the ultimate stereotypical "valley girl," complete with the upspeak to match.

The rise of upspeak since the eighties is well documented in research, and both men and women still use it today.[18] That said, women are twice as likely as men to use it, and we tend to use it in different contexts. Researchers at USC found that women use uptalk as an adaptation to prevent being interrupted, a technique known as floor holding, "the vocal equivalent of holding up your palm, as if to say, 'Wait, I'm not finished!'"[19]

Another theory emerged when researchers took a closer look at how women and men use uptalk on *Jeopardy.* After carefully coding 5,500 responses from three hundred contestants in a hundred episodes of the popular game show, Professor Tom Linneman at William & Mary found the use of uptalk increased significantly among women as they became more successful, joining the show as returning champions. The better they were doing, the more women contestants "softened" their speech with uptalk. Their findings suggest that "women continue to feel they must apologize for their success," says Linneman.[20] The male contestants, on the contrary, used uptalk to signal an actual lack of confidence in their response, when they were truly unsure. The successful women, it appears, might be quite sure of themselves but are putting on a poker face through their vocal tone. Was it a mindless habit or a strategic choice to keep their challengers unsuspecting of their skill? Who's to say for sure?

Here's the bottom line: when you want to come across as more confident and assertive, you're better off kicking upspeak to the curb. Just like eliminating those pesky buzzwords, the best way to start is with a "record and review" session to see whether you're an uptalker in the first place. You can also ask a trusted colleague for feedback. Set him or her up to pay special attention to your way of speaking when you're about to pitch an idea in a meeting, pipe up on a conference call, or give a presentation. Ask that person to watch up for uptalk and give you a subtle cue if he or she catches your intonation going up, up, and away.

Try it!

To practice bringing that upspeak back down, read a news story out loud, and after each declarative sentence say, "damn it!" You can even add a body action—like pounding your fist or stamping your foot—to really help you get your voice back down. As a more public-friendly practice, visualize a gymnast's finish as you speak—like Olympian Simone Biles sticking her landing after flipping her way through a big floor routine. Stick your verbal landing, and you'll speak up *and* sound like a boss.

Visual

Finally, plenty of research shows that your body language has a strong effect on the perception others have of you. When powerful and assertive is the impression you want to give, your walk has to match your talk.

The Eyes Have It

This is one of the simplest but most often overlooked components of body language: What are you *looking* at? Whether you're having a tough conversation with a significant other, pushing back at the negotiation table, or making your case before an audience, you must be able to hold steady eye contact to give an assertive impression.

As the saying goes, "The eyes are the windows to the soul." So, when people see your eyes darting around, they're going to be more likely to suspect you of lying, being nervous, or acting sheepish. Although continuous, prolonged staring is almost universally considered aggressive and threatening, not being comfortable making eye contact at all can leave you looking weak and ashamed—at least here in mainstream Western culture.

A good rule of thumb is to press pause on continuous eye contact about every five seconds in a normal conversation and look up or to the side to indicate that you're thinking. If you're in a full-out debate or want to come off as especially powerful, however, a more consistent gaze can help. Being the first to break eye contact in a tense conversation can be seen as a nonverbal expression of defeat.

When you're speaking up on behalf of yourself or others, holding a steady gaze is key to being seen as calm and confident. Prep by practicing such conversations in the mirror first to see how often your eyes are making contact and to figure out what's triggering you to drop your gaze. Is it when you've got something tough to say? When you're thinking of your next point? When you're feeling nervous?

One trick for making eye contact a little easier is to look *in between* the eyebrows of the person you're addressing. Another that may help is to imagine a triangle between the person's two eyes and mouth and every few seconds adjust where you're looking— first one eye, then the next, then their mouth. When speaking to a crowd of people, you can look at folks' foreheads instead of directly in their eyes if that's easier, too. Just make sure you're varying eye contact regularly between the left, center, and right side of the room.

Open Up, Power Up

The rest of your body position also tells a story—one that can reinforce or contradict the content of your assertive statements. Researchers Dana Carney and Amy Cuddy studied the effect of "high-power" and "low-power" body positions in an experiment designed to test not only how others perceive you, but how you perceive *yourself.*

The concept of high-power body positions is nothing new— they're how most species have always demonstrated dominance: maximizing space and appearing expansive and open. Powerlessness, on the other hand, is expressed through closed, contractive postures, like folding your arms across your chest, crossing and tucking your legs underneath you.

As is usually the case, these power poses have a gendered component. Consider the whole "manspreading" phenomenon of men taking up more space on public transit. The reality is, most of us women have been told since we were little girls to sit like a lady, not take up too much space, and quiet ourselves—in a way that most men just aren't.

Don't believe me? Well, if you're someone who identifies as a woman, I want you to go ahead and try sitting like a man right now. If you're a man, try sitting like a woman. Go ahead. Note that I didn't instruct you on what to do exactly and I can guarantee we all knew what I meant. I bet that men are now sitting cross-legged and prim and women have taken up more space, sometimes a comedic amount of it, too. It's part of the gender performance we've picked up on over the course of our lifetimes.

Or perhaps you don't want to sit like a dude right now for some reason. Are you in public reading this so you don't want to play along? Are you looking over your shoulder to see whether anyone's watching you? Why does it feel so ridiculous for us to be seen acting this way? Because whether they're explicitly stated or not, there are powerful gender norms we're *violating* by simply assuming body positions like these.

Regardless of our gender identity, research shows, much of our body language is innate. One power pose known as the "rockstar" has been seen among blind athletes when they're crossing the finish line in sporting events, throwing their hands up in victory. Even though they've never seen or been taught to strike the pose, raising their arms up wide is something their bodies seem to *want* to do when they're feeling like a winner! It's like we're wired to react in a visceral, physical way when we're feeling powerful.

This is where the research gets interesting. Social scientists have long known that these nonverbal body positions affect how others perceive and feel about us. But the real magic behind Carney and Cuddy's research on power poses is their apparent ability to affect the way *we perceive ourselves.*

Imagine for a moment that you are about to walk into a job interview. You really want the position, but your palms are sweaty and you're nervous that you won't be seen as having enough experience. You want to feel more confident, but your heart is racing out of control and your legs are trembling. Carney and Cuddy found that you can reverse-engineer your body language to produce the courage you desire.

Our actions, even involuntary ones, can influence our self-perception. Studies show that a smile—even an artificial one—can prompt happier emotions. One experiment even suggests that people who use Botox are less prone to anger, perhaps because they can't make angry, frowning faces.[21]

Researchers asked two sets of people to assume high-power poses (like my favorite, the "Wonder Woman") and low-power poses for two minutes and then measured their risk tolerance and body chemistry. After just two minutes, the risk tolerance of the high-power-pose folks soared, and that of the low-power-pose group plummeted. Testosterone—the so-called dominance hormone—rose 20 percent among the high-power-pose group and fell by 10 percent for the low-power-pose group. Cuddy's research reminds me of the simple advice from happiness scholar Gretchen Rubin, who says, "Act the way you want to feel."

Anecdotally, this advice has appeared to work for millions of people who've written in to folks like Cuddy with successful stories of how body language helped them "fake it till you make it." But the power pose findings might actually be more magical than scientific. In a replication study with five times the sample size of the original data set Carney and Cuddy used (which included only forty-two participants), no link was found between power posing and either risk tolerance *or* hormonal changes. But the replication study did confirm that after power posing, participants did *feel* more powerful, and, in my opinion, that positive impact on your self-perception can be power enough to help you gather the courage to assert yourself when it counts.[22]

So, the next time you find yourself needing to draw on your courage to walk into a performance review, nail an interview, or get up in front of your peers for a presentation, remember this: act

ACT THE WAY
you want to feel.

GRETCHEN RUBIN

powerful to feel powerful. Assume a power pose of your choice (the Wonder Woman is my obvious favorite) for at least two minutes, preferably while looking at yourself in the mirror, and you'll walk in with your body language and boosted self-confidence on your side.

Stock Your Toolbox

It's my hope that with these strategies and tactics in your assertive communication toolbox, you won't hesitate the next time you're choosing to advocate for something you believe strongly in. Above all else, remember to focus on your leadership purpose more than the impossible undertaking of perfectly controlling how others perceive you at all times (spoiler alert: it can't be done!). Keep your goals and your audience in mind, and adjust accordingly.

Being comfortable with assertive communication is a key part of getting bossed up. You're the only one who's going to advocate for the life and career you want. You're the one taking the lead on fulfilling your vision. Overcoming roadblocks in your own way doesn't *only* require resilience, it requires the courage to be fiercely assertive on your own behalf, just as you would be on behalf of a loved one or a cause you champion. You, boss, are worthy of that same effort.

Chapter 5

Be a Goal Digger

Now that you're feelin' your boss identity, setting some big audacious goals, and flexing your resilience and assertive communication skills, it's time to take that vision of yours and get very pragmatic. Buckle up, my fellow to-do-list lovers, this is your time to shine.

Why Makin' Boss Moves Is So Hard

Making the shift out of the cycle of burnout to craft a happy, healthy, and sustainable career path is like turning a giant ship around. It's a sea change that doesn't happen overnight. It involves making lots of changes across the spectrum of your work life, your health and wellness, and your relationships. On top of making a major turn in direction, you've also got other roles and responsibilities to juggle and other long-term pursuits you're striving for. This can easily lead you right back into overwhelm if not managed with compassion, resilience, and sound strategy.

Back in my college days I nearly double-majored in cognitive science alongside political science, because I've always been fascinated by the interplay between our individual choices (that we make in our own minds and lives) and how they come together to create our collective culture (the choices that become "the norm" in broader society). I ended up ditching the double-major idea to take five days a week of immersion French-language classes my senior year instead, but that's another story . . .

As it turns out, cognitive science and psychology offer up a wealth of insight relevant to anyone navigating major life changes. One of the first things I did when starting Bossed Up was get back in touch with some of my old cognitive science professors, who then directed me to a listserv of researchers in the field. I emailed the list with a brief description of what I was trying to accomplish with our very first Bossed Up Bootcamp, to see whether anyone thought it aligned with their research and wanted to be a part of it.

That's how I met my now friend and Bossed Up advisory board member Anastasiya Pocheptsova, who earned her PhD studying gender and decision-making at Yale University. Inspired by some of her research on gender and long-term goal attainment, I developed the Bossed Up LifeTracker, a free downloadable e-book and long-term goal-management tool that has helped thousands across the world. It's a simple monthly worksheet specifically designed to sustain focus and motivation over the long term and buffer against the most common roadblocks women experience.

The Head and the Heart

Long-term goals, as it turns out, are such a challenge for us because we humans are of two minds: we all have an emotional side and a logical side. Our emotional mind—or the *heart* of long-term motivation—is critically important in setting off on course to a destination that truly motivates. Like Collins and Porras say in *Built to Last*, our big, hairy, audacious goals are the kind that "hit you in the gut." Those emotional pulls are strong, and that power can be harnessed to create major change in your life.

Equally important, however, is our logical mind—or the head part of motivation—which is thoughtful, analytical, and plan oriented. Many of us Type A folks are more comfortable here, but when the head part of motivation doesn't have a clear destination, or one that really hits us in a powerful, emotional way, we can end up spinning our wheels, drowning in busywork. As Benjamin Franklin, the godfather of personal productivity, said, "Never confuse motion with action."[1]

When the head part of goal pursuit isn't given a clear, compelling direction by our emotional side, we can easily fall into the busy trap of doing, doing, doing, only to look up one day and realize we've been cruising along on a path to someone else's dream life—not the one *we* want for ourselves. Or, worse yet, the need to have an absolutely perfect plan before you proceed might leave you stuck in analysis paralysis, so busy devising the best action plan that you never get around to making a move.

On the other hand, when you lean on the heart alone, it can leave you motivated but unsure of how to proceed, excited for your end goal but unclear on the first steps to make it happen. Perhaps you have a beautiful vision board with a clear picture of your dream life but no plan for achieving it.

Balancing multiple long-term goals requires striking a balance between the head and the heart. Psychologist Jonathan Haidt uses a metaphor to describe this interplay beautifully—the Elephant (representing the heart) and its Rider (representing the head).

Perched atop the Elephant, the Rider holds the reins and seems to be the leader. But the Rider's control is precarious because the Rider is so small relative to the Elephant. Any time the six-ton Elephant and the Rider disagree about which direction to go, the Rider is going to lose. He's completely overmatched.[2]

When you aspire to eat healthier but you find yourself grocery shopping while hungry, the Elephant wins, and you drop that bag of jelly beans into your grocery cart. When you have a savings goal for your retirement fund but those new shoes are too cute to pass up, your Elephant wins. Making peace between our short-term desires and long-term goals isn't just the underlying challenge with achieving our vision, it's the core tug-of-war embedded in our human neurology. But the good news is that you can put them both to work for you. The more we acknowledge and respect the strengths (and weaknesses!) of the Elephant and Rider in our minds, the more likely we are to make our long-term vision a reality.

Chip and Dan Heath, two cognitive scientist brothers, wrote extensively about this interplay in their book *Switch: How to Change When Change Is Hard.*

The Elephant's hunger for instant gratification is the opposite of the Rider's strength, which is the ability to think long-term, to plan, to think beyond the moment (all those things that your pet can't do). . . . The Rider provides the planning and direction, the Elephant provides the energy. A reluctant Elephant or a wheel-spinning Rider accomplishes nothing.[3]

That's why the Heath brothers recommend starting to strategize by taking that grand vision of yours (the one you began to articulate in Chapter 2) and zooming in a bit to picture the near-term future you want, which they call a "Destination Postcard." Whereas your big, audacious goals were focused on where you want to be a decade from now, your Destination Postcard should paint a clear picture of what *could* be possible in the next few months or year. What would making progress on that long-term vision that you would absolutely *love* look like three to six months from now? Or a year from now?

Go ahead and sketch out your Destination Postcard now, following the pattern of brainstorming we did before: work, wellness, love and relationships, and other. In a few sentences or less, where could you be in the near-term future if you were able to make progress toward that long-term vision of yours?

The purpose of a Destination Postcard is to "show the Rider where you're headed and . . . show the Elephant why the journey is worthwhile."[4] For those using the Bossed Up LifeTracker, we ask you to articulate this near-term vision every single month by filling out the vision statements that occupy the left-hand vertical section on the worksheet itself.

Keep in mind, clarifying your vision takes consistent effort—and a little experimentation, too. The more you try on a vision for size (by pursuing it), the more you'll learn along the way whether it's right for you. Think back to the iterative cycle we discussed in Chapter 2—your ambitions may change and evolve. As long as you keep moving, keep striving, and keep checking in with yourself to see how you're feeling along the way, you'll continue to learn what sustainable success looks like *for you.*

Albert Einstein—who knew a *thing or two* about experimentation—echoed these sentiments precisely in a reassuring letter he wrote to his son, Eduard, in which he said, "It is the same with people as it is with riding a bike. Only when moving can one comfortably maintain one's balance."

SPOTLIGHT

"My vision became my guiding compass."

Helen immigrated to the United States from South Korea with her parents at just two years old. They arrived in San Jose, California, with $500 to their name, thanks to the generosity of the congregation where her father served as an administrator, which had taken up a collection to send them off. Helen's father completed only his elementary school education, while her mother's schooling ended in the second or third grade when her own mother passed away.

So you can imagine how big a deal it was a few decades later when Helen not only graduated from college but went on to earn two graduate degrees—one in public administration and another in international relations. Grateful for all her parents had sacrificed for her, Helen pledged to help make life easier for families like hers. That's why she served twice in the US Peace Corps, first in the Republic of Georgia and later in the Philippines.

"It had been a dream of mine ever since I heard of the program in high school. At first, my parents were dead set against it; being the eldest child and only daughter, they thought I was crazy for wanting to go live on the other side of the world and work for free." But, once she was abroad, they saw the work Helen was doing for her village—and they were moved by the parallels between her life abroad and their own lives following the Korean War.

"Adjusting to life abroad gave me a unique insight into my parents' own immigrant experiences—as they had to navigate their new life in America. My Peace Corps experiences also helped me solidify my personal mission: to help vulnerable families so that they can lead healthier, more independent, and sustainable lives."

Years later, as Helen was starting a family of her own, she joined me at Bossed Up Bootcamp, four months pregnant. She'd been working as the senior policy advisor for Congressman Mike Honda, who represented Silicon Valley and who Helen described as "a living legend with such conviction and integrity when it comes to fighting for social justice and civil rights."

Being able to work each and every day on behalf of her deepest-held beliefs was a privilege, and being able to work for her hometown member of Congress who was also a fellow returned Peace Corps volunteer was the ultimate bonus.

But the 2016 elections changed everything for Helen. Not only was she devastated to see Hillary Clinton lose her presidential bid, but she also witnessed her eight-term boss lose that night. She woke up the next day in shock, realizing she was just a few short weeks away from being out of a job.

By this point, Helen's first child was already a year and a half old, and she was expecting another. But, a few weeks after Election Day, Helen learned she'd lost the baby. And, to make matters worse, doctors detected an issue with her thyroid. Reeling from her miscarriage, worried about her pending unemployment, and horrified by the political climate, Helen underwent surgery to remove her thyroid. It was only after its removal that the doctors found otherwise-undetectable cancer cells in her thyroid.

"It was a dark time for me and my family," Helen shared. "But I remember my mother telling me that the child I'd lost had been with me for a reason—to save my life."

After four months of intensive recovery, Helen knew it was time to jump-start her job search. But being out of commission for months had taken its toll. Additionally, once she started interviewing with offices on the Hill again, she found herself running into the same frustrating interview question over and over.

"They'd warn me that work on the Hill can be intense and require long hours," Helen recounted. "They'd say, 'We were here just the other night until 10 p.m., so do you have any outside obligations that might prevent you from doing that?' And I'd respond with, 'Yes, it's called *a family*,' and then I'd remind them that I was a senior staffer in a congressional office for five years, and that included while first becoming a parent and raising a child."

Now more than ever, Helen gained clarity about her job search. Watching out for characteristics that you *don't* want is just as important, if not more, than watching out for those characteristics that you *do* want in your next position. Helen knew that, at the end of the day, her family mattered most—and her next job would have to also fully embrace that.

But shutting the door to job prospects she was qualified for felt scary. They seemed like the natural next step she *should* take, but Helen just couldn't get excited about them. Her internal Rider wanted her to follow the plan and take another job on the Hill, but she couldn't get her inner Elephant to budge. She just could not imagine herself making a job like that work.

Helen reminded herself of her original guiding mission: to help vulnerable families like the one she grew up in. She allowed that vision to serve as her guide as she narrowed down the organizations and offices she would feel comfortable working for. A few weeks later, Helen reconnected with an old colleague who invited her to apply for a position at the Asian & Pacific Islander American Scholarship Fund. She applied, interviewed, and shortly thereafter stepped up as the new director of the Gates Millennium Scholars Program, a job that felt like it was created just for her.

"After just a few weeks on the job, I had the chance to tell my story in a room full of first-generation college students," Helen shared, "and I was completely overcome with emotion. In a way, this job brings me back to who I am—my own identity. I'm working with students whose families are immigrants and struggled economically, socially, and culturally—just like mine. As refugees, some of them underwent even greater obstacles. And through it all, they have this deep understanding of the role that education can play in bettering their lives, their communities, and even honoring their ancestors. I am a living testament to that."

Throughout the total of eight months she spent out of work, Helen relied on that original mission for her life to serve as her guiding compass. It's what led her to this new position helping vulnerable families become healthier, more sustainable, and more independent through education. She was especially thrilled with it because she was now in a family-first work culture. Her new colleagues all recognized their work was important, impactful, and life changing, but personal sustainability was a priority. That facet became instrumental three months into her new job, when Helen's mom got into a frightening and life-threatening car accident.

"While I was heartbroken to leave behind my husband and two-year-old son in DC, I had no choice but to take a leave of absence to go and take care of my mom," Helen remembered.

"I went to California to serve as my mom's translator and her primary caregiver for months. I'm so grateful I was able to be there for her and have my job waiting for me upon return."

Three months later, with her mom's health stabilized, Helen returned to work and has been thriving there ever since. She's more confident than ever that she made the right choice.

"I'm so glad I stayed true to the values that had been driving my career all along," said Helen, "and I'm now able to make taking care of myself and my family a priority in a whole new way."

Since the beginning of this year, as part of this commitment, she's slowly taken the time and effort for more self-care, and as she sees it, family care. As her own mother put it, "A healthy mom is a healthy family." She's adopted a regular exercise routine, meditates daily, seeks out acupuncture, and has even incorporated a whole new skin care routine.

"As ridiculous as a fifteen-minute skincare regimen sounds," Helen laughed, "it's so worth it! When I feel good, I'm better able to show up for my family *and* my work. Learning to take that holistic view on my vision for my life and career continues to be part of how I'm creating my own peace."

Break It Down

Although clarifying your vision and Destination Postcard is important, it's not sufficient. In fact, focusing too much on the end goal (instead of the journey you'll take to achieve it) can have unintended negative effects.

Researchers from the University of California tested the power of vision in two forms: envisioning yourself achieving your goal (in this case, acing a test) and envisioning yourself taking the actions that would help you achieve it (like studying for the test).[5] Students were broken into three groups. One was asked to imagine themselves acing the test, the second to make a plan as to how they were going to ace the test, and the third was not given any exercise at all.

Researchers found that students in the second group who focused on *the process* not only performed the best overall but also studied more and experienced "reduced anxiety" on test day when compared to their peers. The students who focused on the *outcome,* envisioning themselves acing the test, performed worst overall— even worse than the students who had not been asked to envision anything! Scientists theorized that too much focusing on the outcomes of your vision (i.e., all the cutting and pasting of your dream house, dream job, and dream vacation that go into a fancy "vision board") can actually leave you worse off because your brain starts to feel as though you've already achieved it. Yikes.

So all that "dream it and you'll achieve it" advice you may have heard over the years? It's time to drop that way of thinking that conflates *confidence* with *preparation and planning.* Focusing on the journey ahead—not just the end destination—leaves you more likely to achieve your goals and helps maintain your motivation over time, especially through that middle dip in motivation. Researchers found that our drive is highest at the starting line of setting a new goal and toward the end once the finish line is within sight. That middle slog of the journey? Well, that's where our motivation takes a big dip.[6]

So let's say you set a long-term goal that will take six months to achieve, like training for a half marathon. A six-month-long goal means that your middle dip is going to be quite long—your motivation might be stuck in the mud for a few *months* there, not just days or weeks. But you can actually trick yourself into reducing the duration of the middle dip by focusing on achieving smaller action steps—subgoals—along the way.

So instead of focusing on your six-month goal to run a half marathon, which might seem entirely impossible to you at the outset, focus this week on your goal to run three miles. This week's long run (of three miles) becomes the finish line you're focused on all week, and your middle dip lasts only a day or two in the middle of the week. So when you wake up on Wednesday and don't feel like getting out of bed and slipping into your sneakers, at least you know your motivation will be back on track within a few days—not months—because you're striving for your end goal on Saturday. Bring your finish line closer! Focus on how you're going to act day to day, week to week to propel yourself forward.

As you focus on closer-term "finish lines" week after week, not only does your motivation dip less, but you also stay focused on the progress you're making. And, remember, the perception of progress alone is inherently motivating! I used this exact strategy myself when I set out to conquer my first-ever 5K race all the way through training for my first (and, let's be honest, probably my last) Olympic triathlon and was emotionally boosted by setting new personal records each and every week! Your confidence soars when you stay focused on small wins—not a seemingly impossible finish line that's months away.

Setting a clear Destination Postcard is a way to bring the finish line closer on any of those audacious ten-year goals you have in mind. So, let's take that another step further. What are the concrete next steps you need to make your Destination Postcard a reality? What could you do today? This week? This month? How can you move the finish line closer on the Destination Postcard itself?

The Rider in your head is awaiting your orders—so script your next move, boss! Let's get into the nitty-gritty now. Unpack big bundled action steps like "grow my network" into concrete, measurable actions like:

- ✸ Go to two networking events each month.
- ✸ Have one coffee meeting with a colleague each week.
- ✸ Email my former boss or professor to see whether she knows anyone in the field I should connect with.

Don't get too bogged down in analyzing how many of these steps are *possible* or *practical* in this phase, just get all the concrete, measurable action steps you can possibly think of out of your head so you can be strategic in how to approach them next. It's true that all these action steps can get overwhelming quickly when there are lists upon lists running through your mind, but, before you can sort them out, you need all your cards on the table.

Shake It Out

Before you dive into execution, get *all* the possible next action steps out of your head and onto the page in a loose, free-for-all brainstorm.

1. Think back to your Destination Postcard to remind yourself where you're headed in each of the categories of goals

you have right now (pertaining to work, wellness, love and relationships, and other).

2. Then set yourself five whole minutes on the timer to shake out all your ideas for action steps that might bring you closer to that destination on a piece of scratch paper. And I mean *all* your possible action steps: Big ones. Little ones. Easy ones. Hard ones. Action steps you're not quite sure you're going to take and those you know you can tackle right now.

3. Phone a friend if you need to. If you're not a list-making fanatic, or just feel like there's this black hole between where you are and where you want to be, this can be the trickiest part. And the more complex your goals become (like, say, getting a promotion), the murkier the path to getting there can be. That's why this is a brainstorm you should engage in *with others* whenever possible. In fact, in the next section, when we talk about developing a community of people you can strive *and* thrive with, this is a fundamental part of those relationships: helping lift each other up on your journey to living a boss life.

Once they're all out on the page, we can move on to prioritizing them.

Fast Things First

In our rapidly accelerating society, I firmly believe that focus is a better predictor of success than hard work or intelligence alone. How do you bring focus to your life when there are so many things you want to accomplish? You have to set your priorities.

It sounds simple, and it is, in theory. But, in practice, you're bound to be yanked, pulled, and stretched to make other people's priorities *your* priorities. Guarding your time is part of the reason you'll need those assertive communication skills and resilience to help you take the lead in determining how you spend your time.

To make all those action steps you just wrote down less over-whelming, you have to highlight the priorities you want to focus on first. **Highlighting** is a goal management strategy that in-volves the *temporary* prioritization of certain goals over others. By no means are we abandoning those other to-do list items for very long, but it does mean there will be certain goals in your life you are not actively engaged with at times, so as to provide time and energy to focus on other goals. That way you're able to bring a singular, laser-like focus to one effort at a time. This mono-tasking approach is essential—and something that studies show can be difficult for women in particular.

Women tend to experience more goal conflict in our lives (leading to feelings of role overload, as we discussed in Chapter 1) and are likely to be actively engaged in more goals at once than men. Women are more likely to try to accomplish multiple things at once than our male counterparts, and we tend to generalize in many pursuits instead of specializing in any given one.[7]

As such, we experience more internal conflict and guilt as we try to parse our priorities, especially with goals that are relational. When we want to be a "good boss" and a "good mom" and a "good wife," we find our identities fractured, and our time starts to feel minced into "time confetti," as author Brigid Schulte calls it.

Mindful, proactive prioritization can help. So now that you've dumped all your ideas for next steps out onto the page, go through and numerically order them according to priority across each category (so there is a number one priority in each of the four areas: work, wellness, love and relationships, and other).

Here are a few research-based best practices to keep in mind as you go:

1. Start with the Quick and Easy

The mere act of getting things done is intrinsically motivating. Progress begets progress. So start with the easy stuff!

The "progress principle," as it's known in the research, shows that, when pursuing a goal, nothing boosts your motivation like making forward movement on meaningful work. "The more frequently people experience that sense of progress," write Teresa Amabile and Steven Kramer in the *Harvard Business Review,* "the more likely they are to be creatively productive in the long run."[8] So give yourself a head start by making it easy to check the first few items off your list.

2. Strive for Strategic Overlap

Unlike multitasking, **strategic overlap** means you can make progress on multiple goals with a single action. So, instead of trying to cook dinner (one action) and read more business books (a totally different action), which don't pair well, you might go running with a friend to make progress on both your wellness goals and your relationship goals with a single action. Or perhaps you walk to work while listening to your favorite daily news podcast, so you're able to stay informed *and* get in those steps while commuting. Look for opportunities to "feed two birds with one seed," so to speak.

3. Try Temptation Bundling

Temptation bundling is like strategic overlap, but it takes the concept one step further by pairing up an action you're taking to move toward your goal with an indulgence![9] Temptation bundling is all about allowing the Elephant to have its way with its short-term desires (I want to veg out and watch trashy reality TV!) by combining it with an action that helps you make progress on your goals (I'll watch from the stationary bike in the gym!). So it's a little bit of #treatyoself moment combined with a productive action step.

One of your wellness goals might be that you want to drink more water to stay hydrated. But what does the Elephant in your head always want? Coffee! At least that's true if you're like me—a bit of a coffee fanatic. So with the help of temptation bundling, I came up with a new rule for myself: I have to have a whole glass of water every single time I pour myself a cup of coffee. Once I've linked the two actions into a habit, it becomes easier to just put it on autopilot. Pour yourself a coffee? Pour yourself a glass of water. By connecting the two actions, you're actually using the anchor action that your Elephant is always wanting anyway (Coffee! Coffee! Coffee!) with the progress you want to make on your wellness goal (Water!).

Look for opportunities to connect the action steps you want to take with rewards you'll find motivating for the most impactful "bundle" that will keep your motivation high. Mind you, these work best when the indulgence is *not* something that completely contradicts your ultimate goal (buying expensive trinkets wouldn't be a great indulgence to pair with action steps related to saving money, for instance), but as we see with the coffee example above, even a "two steps forward, one step back" strategy works as long as it keeps up your motivation to continue in pursuit of your goal.

4. Capitalize on the Fresh Start Effect

When using the Bossed Up LifeTracker, you'll reset your priorities and action steps with a fresh new worksheet at the start of every single month. I also highly encourage our users to take a moment on Sunday nights or Monday mornings to take stock of the week ahead and figure out when and how you'll take action on your priority goals each week. This is no coincidence.

Researchers have found that "salient temporal landmarks" immediately increase our motivation to take action on our goals. When we feel like we've arrived at the start of something new—Monday, the first of the month, the New Year, or even our birthday—we're more likely to "take a big-picture view of [our] lives, and thus motivate aspirational behaviors."[10]

So tap into your motivation when it's at its natural peaks—at the start of the year, month, and week. Make a habit of reviewing your goals, priorities, and action steps at these critical times, and you'll sustain your progress over the long term.

Prioritizing *proactively* can help prepare you for when the whirlwind of everyday life takes hold and it becomes hard to find time to make progress on your big, audacious goals. Hold tight to your growth mindset, your grit, and resilience, and be open to constantly iterating your roadmap to make your vision a reality.

As you begin to make progress, you'll inevitably learn more about *how* to move forward strategically and add more action steps to your ever-growing list. Just remember the power of prioritization to bring focus to your journey ahead.

SPOTLIGHT

"It helped me feel in control."

Jonelle is a marketing professional whose love for great television and film led her to the Big Apple to start her career in publicity and marketing.

But, after two years working in a brand marketing role, Jonelle felt like her career was coasting. Work was, well, fine. But *just* fine. In fact, Jonelle was starting to feel like she was going through the motions and getting complacent. She was thirsting for growth, and, when the New Year came along, she harnessed that fresh start and made a resolution to start a job search for a new, challenging opportunity that would reignite that fire in her belly she once had for her work.

"I felt like I could have coasted in that role forever," said Jonelle, "but I wanted to wake up and feel engaged in my work, so I had to find a way to make searching for another job important, even when, frankly, it wasn't urgent."

A Bossed Up Bootcamp alumna, Jonelle was familiar with the Bossed Up LifeTracker and printed one out each month and inserted it into her day planner so she could keep her long-term goals top of mind. In fact, it was bosses like her who inspired me to launch our own LifeTracker Planner a few years ago!

"Mapping out my job search helped me feel more in control," Jonelle told me. "I broke things down into measurable action steps for each month that helped me reduce my anxiety over something as uncertain as a long job search."

She set out numerical objectives for each month:

1. Attend three networking events
2. Apply to four jobs a week
3. Meet with one contact for coffee each week

"Checking those off gave me such satisfaction and provided me a sensation of forward momentum," Jonelle shared, "and that was especially important when I'd sometimes go an entire month without getting called in for an interview. Instead of feeling totally unaccomplished, I could look at my LifeTracker and remind myself of all the effort I'd put in and everything that I'd learned along the way."

The reality is, there's only so much you can control. You can polish up your resume, you can do the work of applying to jobs and networking like a champ, but there's an element of patience inherent to any career transition, as you wait for the right opportunity to reveal itself.

"Breaking things down helped focus my efforts and keep me afloat," said Jonelle.

After all, Jonelle wasn't trying to run *from* a job, she wanted to find a job worth running *toward.* She had a day job that was paying the bills just fine, but that meant she had to check job boards each morning before starting her day, drag herself to networking events at night, and spend weekends preparing applications.

"To be honest, my life didn't look super 'balanced' at that time," said Jonelle, "but it was a deliberate priority I set, and I'm glad that I made that choice."

Jonelle mindfully highlighted her job search and prioritized that over other objectives in her life. She didn't make her social life or wellness regimen the top priority for those few months, but she also knew that it wasn't going to be that way forever. She gave herself permission to drive hard on her job search, even though she had her low points.

"There were definitely nights when I didn't feel like doing the work," confessed Jonelle. "I mean, it is like having a second job on top of your full-time job! But I bounced back from those dips by just refocusing at the start of the next month when I reorganized my plan and refreshed my LifeTracker."

All that perseverance and focus was starting to pay off, too. At one point, Jonelle was called in for eight separate interviews in one week! Though they didn't all go perfectly, she used those experiences as practice and learned from them until, finally, she found herself weighing multiple job offers from one of her dream employers: a major children's television network. She leapt at the opportunity to try her hand in a new kind of role in partnership marketing.

"It scared me—but in a good way," Jonelle told me. "It was a new path and would require me to step up to the plate and learn a lot of new skills on the job. It would be a great learning opportunity and maybe even a launchpad for the rest of my career."

All in, Jonelle's job search lasted just over eight months. That's not an easy amount of time to sustain your motivation and pursue a goal that, although important, isn't inherently urgent. But Jonelle is so happy she persisted—and is now approaching the rest of her life with that same deliberate strategy.

"My job is so exciting, and I love having such a big influence over our major marketing campaigns," said Jonelle, "but now I'm going back and applying that same strategy to my health and wellness goals."

Just like she didn't always want to drag herself to nightly networking events, Jonelle still has a hard time finding the motivation to make it to her 6:30 a.m. spin classes, but she's setting herself up with a plan to maintain her forward momentum. She's once again breaking down big health goals into concrete action steps that help her sustain her progress.

"And when I feel like I don't know what's next or feel like my motivation is low," Jonelle reported, "I revisit my plan, break things down into subgoals, and everything feels immediately more doable."

Quit Some Sh*t

Another way to keep overwhelm at bay? *Just quit it.*

I see time and again that women are so much more likely to fall into the "Jack of all trades, master of none" lifestyle that they might as well change it to "Jane of all trades, master of none."

I get it. You're a multi-passionate person. Who isn't?! My big life goals include running a successful international business, having a family, maybe owning and operating a bakery someday, and probably running for office. But am I pursuing all of those giant ambitions at the same time? Hell, no! Are those goals bound to adjust and shift along the way? Of course.

When you want to make big changes in your life—you want to change industries, you want to start a business, you want a promotion and raise, you want to stop dating jerks, you want to get in the best shape of your life—you're going to need to make that change a priority. It's going to require a *lot* of your limited time and energy, and if you're like most of us, you're going to have to juggle that priority with the kinds of obligations that keep your lights on and bills paid. So if you're pursuing five different goals at any given time and some of them just don't seem to be working, no matter what you try, no matter how much you pivot or persevere, maybe it's time to quit it.

Is your time swallowed up by activities you feel you must do out of obligation or guilt or for the sake of conformity? Maybe you can sit this year's bake sale out. Are there things you're doing because you think you *should* like them—even though you don't? Maybe Pilates isn't right for you.

There are major downsides to the philosophy that "a winner never quits and quitters never win." Economists know this best. We have to weigh our "sunk costs"—all that time, effort, money, and resources we've already poured into an endeavor—right alongside our "opportunity costs"—what you may be missing out on because you're in pursuit of said goal.

Only you can decide when quitting is the right call. But consider this: if after a few months a goal, relationship, or career path you're actively pursuing isn't actually bringing you closer to that audacious vision you set for your life, that might be reason enough.

When it's the right call for you, don't be afraid to drop it like it's hot and quit like a boss.

Proactive Versus Reactive

Being a goal digger is all about making the act of focusing on your ambitions into a practice. When it comes to bringing about big changes in your life, there's an enormous difference between feeling *proactive* (like a leader) and *reactive* (like a victim). Are you behind the wheel or in the passenger's seat? All the tactics we've discussed as well as the Bossed Up LifeTracker are designed to help us take a proactive approach, but, of course, life has a way of throwing chaos into our path.

A call from the doctor we didn't see coming. A loved one suddenly in need of our support. A new opportunity . . . halfway across the globe. There are lots of unforeseeable changes that will throw a wrench into the best-laid plans. But being a boss is all about how you *react* to that chaos—either with compassion for yourself or with stress and guilt.

Earlier this year I went home to my parents' house outside Hartford, Connecticut, to attend the bridal shower of my best friend from my earliest days of childhood. This was my first time serving as a maid of honor, and I was so excited to come home and celebrate with such a dear, lifelong friend. The morning of the brunch reception, my dad asked me whether I'd be able to spare a little time to talk through a situation he was facing at work. Because negotiation and assertive communication are topics I read, think, and talk about often, of course I wanted to be there for my dad! He has this really self-deprecating way of asking me for time, too, laying on a guilt trip like only a Jewish father can by saying, "Do ya think you'll have a little time to spare for your dear old dad this visit?"

I had originally planned to go for a run that morning, because I was feeling antsy and desperate for a sweat session to calm my stress after a long and hectic week of travel. When I expressed the idea, my mom wanted in, too, but proposed a walk with the dog in lieu of a run. It was less than the kind of stress-busting cardio exercise I was looking for, but, as my mom reminded me, the dog needed to be walked before we left, and if she didn't do it, "No one else will."

Thinking back on what I know about strategic overlap, I suggested that Dad come along with us and we could talk and walk through his negotiation scenario together as we walked with Mama and the dog.

Although the dog ended up getting walked, my mom got some exercise, and my dad and I continued the negotiation conversation for over an hour upon arriving back home, the only thing I didn't get were my own needs met. Was that a workout for me? No. Were my stress levels any lower? Quite the contrary.

And now, to top it all off, I was going to be late to my best friend's bridal shower, the first of all the wedding events. I quickly hopped in the shower and resorted to crappily doing my makeup in the car on the way, feeling like a total teary-eyed, mascara-smeared mess and a terrible maid of honor.

Granted, this was just one little morning dealing with a very privileged set of problems, but it's illustrative of the kind of role overload we all face on a daily or weekly basis when we get in the habit of mindlessly saying yes to everyone else before we say yes to our own needs. It adds up. I wanted to be a present daughter, a good bridesmaid, and a dedicated runner all at once. Despite my best intentions, I felt reactive instead of proactive. I felt like I'd given up my agency in the situation, like I hadn't been assertive about guarding my boundaries, and it left me feeling frustrated, resentful—*and* guilty for feeling that way!

What would have made this situation better? A mindful commitment to being proactive. No matter how good our intentions, we can't negotiate with the space-time continuum itself. So, instead, we must negotiate the expectations of ourselves and others. Looking back I wish I'd said to my father, "Yes! I am so down to talk through this negotiation situation, but I want to give that my full attention, so let's have that conversation this afternoon over coffee."

Then maybe I could have walked the dog with mom as a warm-up and made time for my very necessary stress-busting run. Or perhaps taken the dog with me on my run *for* mom. But being assertive with those we love is sometimes even harder than having tough conversations with our colleagues (like Loryn's spotlight in the last chapter taught us). And being proactive is easier said than done in the face of life's chaos.

These skills are muscles we can all develop over time, without having to be perfect about it. It's all about being able to take a step back, draw deeply on our courage and self-worth, our boss identity and assertive communication skills, and say when and how we will reshuffle our priorities for the various roles we play in relation to others.

SPOTLIGHT

"I try to master one thing at a time."

After working for ten years in finance, Eva had a padded paycheck, but she had left her dreams and passions completely unattended. Ever since she was a child, Eva had a passion for food and wished she could spend all day in the kitchen. At age thirty-two, she finally decided to experiment with her lifelong dream by going to culinary school on the side, and she began exploring what a major career shift in that direction might look like.

"Culinary school was a challenge because I wasn't eighteen years old and my classmates were mostly young men. But I didn't let being an outlier bog me down or distract from my focus," said Eva. "During my time there, I completed a beautiful portfolio and business plan. The day after graduation, I decided to make the leap, leave the finance world, and launch my personal chef business."

Eva set out with an ambitious five-year plan for growing her culinary empire, which centered on helping people heal through easy access to healthy, nutrient-rich food.

"The biggest thing for me was taking that entire five-year vision and breaking it up into yearly, monthly, and even then weekly goals," said Eva. "And when the going got tough, I had to remind myself of the big vision I was striving toward."

At Bossed Up Bootcamp she connected with other women navigating career transitions and made a new friend, Doreen, who would end up playing an instrumental role as her accountability buddy in the months and years that followed.

"We ended up creating so much together," Eva shared. "We collaborated, we held each other accountable to our biggest goals, and we cheered each other on when troubleshooting new ideas and solving problems that arose."

Eva is a self-proclaimed "ideas person," always scheming and dreaming up another big plan. For her, follow-through wasn't always easy, and having strategies to maintain her motivation through its natural dips was key. As a total people person, Eva could get lonesome after long days in the kitchen preparing client meals, so when she wasn't feeling super motivated, she'd rely on the reward of investing in herself further. She frequently attended conferences, took online courses, and joined friends for a night out when a speaker they admired came to town.

"Personal development is so huge for me," Eva acknowledged, "because I feel my best when I know I'm making progress."

She went on to complete a certification in plant-based culinary medicine and transitioned her business to a 100 percent plant-based personal chef service, always striving to further the health and well-being of her clients. And when she and her husband relocated from Virginia to Florida, Eva evolved the business again to focus on lifestyle and wellness coaching, specifically for women who struggle with food-related stress and self-care.

Throughout it all, Eva was certain that focusing on one objective at a time was key to her long-term success, even through multiple evolutions of her business.

"It's all about breaking the big goal down into bite-size pieces," she said. "And that's hard for me sometimes because I have so many ideas I want to pursue, but I really try to master *one* thing at a time and stay focused on a daily accomplishment."

With a step-by-step plan and a strong accountability system in place, Eva's business was cash-flow positive after the first year, and she's gained so much more along the way—including an expanded outlook on what she sees as possible for her future.

"I really used to feel like I needed to do it all myself," she told me, "and that took me so much longer to accomplish the things I wanted to. Now I realize how much more you can achieve when you're open to collaborate. People *are* willing to help you make things bigger and better. People *are* willing to hold you accountable. My squad of support is what's helped make my planning and execution so much stronger."

Your Calendar = Your Budget for Life

One tool that's been tremendously helpful for bringing more intention to my life is my calendar. Since launching Bossed Up and working with thousands of other women on this, I've started using my calendar differently than I did before.

At the start of each week, I look at the action items on my LifeTracker to review what I'm actively pursuing across work, wellness, love and relationships, and anything else. I estimate how long each of those action items will take and plot them out on my daily calendar for the week ahead. At a glance, I can get a sense of where there may be trouble spots (if I've got too much scheduled hour by hour for every second of a given day, for instance) and where there might be some free time I can use to reshuffle things. As my week progresses, if I have to skip a friend date or a workout I had scheduled, it's already on the calendar, so I make a point to reschedule it just like I would reschedule any work obligation that got pushed around. In this way I'm using my calendar as **a forecasting tool** to be proactive with my goal management.

Conversely, at the end of each week and month, I like to look back at my calendar to see what worked and where I struggled. On Friday afternoons if I'm feeling particularly overcommitted, stressed-out, or overwhelmed, I can look for evidence as to what may have caused it by looking back on my calendar. Often the culprit is that I chronically underestimate the time it'll take for me to accomplish a given task. I call this **aspirational planning,** and it's a bad habit that leads to unintentionally overcommitting myself, one I'm actively working to kick to the curb. Do you find yourself doing the same?

But by reviewing my calendar at the end of each week and month, I'm essentially able to use it as an **assessment tool** as well. This helps me work smarter along the way and learn which tasks I need to budget more time for in the future. This helps me forecast better the next week and normalize my calendar so that it's less aspirational and more realistic.

Your calendar is just like a budget—but instead of chronicling your important financial resources, it tracks an even more finite one: your time. The boundaries we set (in our calendar *and* budgets, for that matter) are a reflection of our values. So don't tell me you value staying active outdoors or spending time with family—give me your calendar and I'll tell you what you value. It's not about what you *will* do, or what you *would* do, it's what you *do*.

Setting those boundaries with compassion—for the ones you love and for yourself—is the literal fight for your life. Guard your time. Keep your heart engaged with the big picture, and use your head to set realistic strategies for achieving it, step by step.

The good news is, you don't have to go it alone.

Chapter 6

Your Community of Courage

I consider myself a bit of a lone wolf. Always have been. I never had a large gaggle of girlfriends and always secretly thought that if I wanted to pursue extraordinary success it would mean taking "the road less traveled" and, well, walking it alone.

At the very start of this book, after all, we focused on the most important first step of getting bossed up: seeing yourself as the leader of your own life. But here's what I've come to learn: seeing yourself as a boss is easier when you're surrounded by other people who reinforce it. Our identities aren't shaped solely in our own heads (unless you're a clinical narcissist with zero empathy). We become leaders through that iterative process, remember? We take purposeful action, gauge the reaction we see *from others,* and then internalize that response. Developing your boss identity is far from a solitary endeavor: it hinges on being surrounded by people who see you as the person you want to be.

Mirrors Matter

This is especially critical when you're pushing your limits and expanding the capacity you believe you have to create a new, bolder, more courageous life. When you're interviewing for a huge new promotion, deciding to walk away from a long-term relationship, or moving solo across the globe. What you need during these moments of **identity expansion** is someone who believes in you as much as—if not *more* than—you believe in yourself.

It's the reason I was able to run that half marathon: my running buddies believed I could do it before I realized I could. It's the reason I was able to persevere through the most challenging early days of launching my business: my advisory board and, yes, my boo believed in my vision and in my ability to make it a reality even when I was feeling like a fraud.

There are always going to be days when you find it hard to tap into your boss identity. When you go to call upon your reserves of courage and resilience, only to hit the bottom of the barrel. No one person has unshakeable confidence, and anyone who pretends otherwise is just dealing in shallow bravado, not that deep, inner, calm confidence that's so essential for sustainable success. It's in those moments that we must turn to those we trust for identity reinforcement.

I call this **mirror theory**: you're better able to cultivate a boss identity when surrounded by a community of people who mirror back *to you* the most courageous reflection of who you can be. You know how some mirrors make you look a little better than others? And some are just downright fun-house mirrors that completely warp the image you see of yourself? People are the same way.

It's not that anyone's necessarily trying to reflect back some messed-up image of who you are and who you can become; it's just that we humans often get stuck in our own heads and project our baggage onto each other. It's why so many folks find working with a coach or therapist helpful: they are specially trained to hold up a helpful, less biased reflection to support their clients' self-exploration.

But don't get it twisted—there's nothing magical about mirror theory. Your community can't *carry* you. It doesn't know what kinds of mirrors you need and when. It's up to you to stand in front of the mirrors you need when you're looking for confidence, courage, and support in achieving your big dreams.

My dad, for instance, with his brilliant, analytical, lawyerly mind, is an expert at figuring out everything that could possibly go wrong. He's so good at zoning in on risks, however, that sometimes he can reflect back to me my deepest worries, anxieties, and fears. Does he do this intentionally? Absolutely not. Does he still love me unconditionally? You bet.

But when I'm feeling insecure, full of self-doubt, and worrying that maybe I'm a fool to be trying this scary new thing, he's not the first guy I call. You cannot go back and stand in front of fun-house mirrors time and again and hope to see something less freaky. Well, I suppose you can spend your whole life hoping that those mirrors will straighten out, but you risk losing touch with your boss identity along the way. I happen to believe it's a lot more effective to find some new mirrors instead.

Now when I'm daring to take big risks and need some courage and practical advice, I call my brilliant college bestie, my boo, or fellow entrepreneurs who've been around the block before. I've learned to assertively seek out the kind of feedback and advice I need in a more targeted way, and take responsibility for not just calling the first folks who come to mind but, rather, thinking critically about what kind of perspective I need in the moment.

The bottom line is: the people we surround ourselves with *matter*. They contribute to our very identities that make up who we are.

SPOTLIGHT

"I'd been seeing myself through the eyes of my last boss."

At twenty-five, Sarah found herself feeling trapped in a job that had turned toxic. It was her first post out of college, a coordinator role at a national nonprofit, and Sarah was devoted to the organization. But, after three years of proving herself, she was essentially performing the tasks of a manager without the compensation or title to accompany the responsibility. Naturally, when a new vacancy opened up, Sarah—with the support and sponsorship of senior colleagues—was vying for a promotion through HR.

For months she waited to hear back about scheduling a time for her interview, only to learn from another colleague that HR had been interviewing external candidates. Sarah was taken aback but checked in to ensure she was still in the running. Despite stringing her along, HR hadn't bothered to circle back with Sarah (not to mention affording her the opportunity to interview) until after the new hire was made.

"I felt patronized, disrespected, and like all my devotion to the organization counted for nothing," Sarah said. "But I was so bought into our mission and vision, even *looking* elsewhere felt like cheating."

Feeling deflated and foolish for focusing solely on investing in an organization that clearly wasn't investing in her, Sarah knew she needed out. The stress of chronic overwork coupled with feeling completely undervalued had taken its toll, and Sarah's anxiety was spiraling out of control. She found herself crying on the Metro every morning as she desperately tried to will herself in to work each day.

The year prior, Sarah attended Bossed Up Bootcamp, where she got clear on her ultimate career goal: to lead a national nonprofit from the C-suite. With her long-term vision in sight, she could no longer tolerate wasting time at what had become a dead-end job, where she felt her employer saw her only in her entry-level capacity.

With some savings to fall back on and the privilege of being able to ask her parents for help, Sarah tendered her resignation without having her next job lined up. She hated asking her folks for support after being financially independent since graduation, but her burnout had come to a head, and she knew she needed to make a change fast. "Being able to lean on them was a total privilege, I know," Sarah admitted, "but I'm so glad I didn't let my pride get in the way. I needed their help, and asking for it is part of what propelled me forward."

In the six months that followed, Sarah found herself in a grueling job search. She kept making it to the final round of interviews, only for the position to ultimately go to someone else. I sat down with Sarah during this time to help review her approach and quickly realized something: she was aiming too low.

She'd been so used to being seen as an entry-level coordinator, Sarah was applying to jobs of a comparable scope—ones she could easily knock out of the park, she figured. She had been so worn down by her last workplace, Sarah wasn't seeing herself as capable of anything more. In other words, she was stuck seeing herself in warped fun-house mirrors.

I pushed her to consider what a growth position would look like instead. If her ultimate goal was to lead a nonprofit, Sarah was going to need a lot of managerial experience. Because she didn't have any previously, Sarah figured that would be something to aim for in the job *after* this next job. I asked her why: Why wasn't she explicitly focusing on jobs that would enable her to rise to the occasion *now?* That way, this next move would be a clear stepping-stone on her path to achieving her ultimate goal. But, to make that happen, she had to believe in her ability to rise to such an occasion first.

"I remember you saying to me, 'No, you are going to be managing people in your next job,'" Sarah recently recounted to me, "and that's when I started to believe in that possibility."

Once Sarah was more specifically articulating that she was looking for a step up from the entry-level position she'd already proven herself more than capable in, her story resonated more with people. Out at networking events and in informational interviews, people responded to her progress-oriented come-up narrative, and they admired the drive and ambition underlying it.

"Previously, I'd been seeing myself through the eyes of my last boss," Sarah said, "instead of the kind of person I wanted my next boss to be: someone who believed I was capable of more."

A few months later, a new contact Sarah met at a networking happy hour mentioned a local nonprofit that was hiring. That lead turned into a referral, that referral turned into an interview, and before she knew it, Sarah was negotiating her official offer for the role of manager of foundation relations, which included managing her first direct report!

"There were so many moments when I doubted myself," Sarah confessed, "even *after* I took the job!"

She was, after all, managing for the first time *and* managing someone who was more seasoned in her career and had more experience. For a young, first-time manager, that growth curve can be steep.

"But I'm also fortunate to be able to go to *my* manager for support, too," said Sarah. "I'm fortunate to work for someone now who's really invested in my growth."

Looking back, Sarah said she hopes more women can see themselves as capable of growth in leaps and bounds from the get-go—or at least with a little help from their community of courage.

"The biggest thing I learned by far," Sarah told me recently, "is not to be afraid to make a jump when you're not happy. It's okay to look elsewhere. It's okay to interview. It's okay to leave! You're well within your rights and shouldn't be afraid to explore your opportunities to grow elsewhere."

Shine Together

Cultivating a strong community of women who support one another has been a key part of getting bossed up for so many women I work with—and for me! But unfortunately there's the stupid stereotype out there that women don't like to help other women. That we're catty and gossipy and likely to claw out each other's eyes on our rise to the top. There's this idea that, in our male-dominated world, there can only be a few fierce females on top, and that scarcity means extra competition among women.

This idea of the office "queen bee" was described by Marianne Cooper in the *Atlantic* as "the successful woman who instead of using her power to help other women advance, undermines her women colleagues."[1] Have you run into a queen bee or two in your time? It's totally possible. But know this: she's the exception—not the rule. A wealth of research shows that the "queen bee" myth is an outdated idea to retire alongside shoulder pads and fax machines. It might have been big in the past, but it's passé.

Sheryl Sandberg and Adam Grant dished out the facts on this matter in another one of their *New York Times* op-eds:

> In business and in government, research supports the notion that women create opportunities for women. On corporate boards, despite having stronger qualifications than men, women are less likely to be mentored—unless there's already a woman on the board. And when women join the board, there's a better chance that other women will rise to top executive positions. We see a similar pattern in politics: In Latin America between 1999 and 2013, female presidents appointed 24 percent more female ministers to their cabinets than the average for their region.[2]

The misconception that women *don't* help other women is likely due to our dear old friend that keeps popping up: unconscious gender bias. When men battle it out at work, they're seen as competitive but collegial. We're accustomed to thinking of men as competitive—no big deal. But when women engage in the same kind of day-to-day disagreement? They're perceived as "Mean Girls locked in a heated catfight," says Marianne Cooper.[3]

One study demonstrated this perfectly by having two groups of people read a story about two colleagues engaged in a conflict at work.[4] When women's names were used, the readers determined the conflict to be more damaging to the relationship and assumed there would be more long-term negative consequences. When men's names were used (but everything else about the story remained identical), participants didn't think the conflict would be such a big deal. It seems that we unconsciously "problematize" conflict between women in the workplace in a way we don't for men, making much ado about nothing.

So don't get bogged down in this "queen bee" BS. Instead, I subscribe to what Anne Friedman calls **shine theory:** the belief that kickass women who team up with other kickass women help shine an even brighter spotlight on one another.[5] It's the underlying principle behind the idea that bossed up women *lift as we climb.*

"I don't shine if you don't shine," says Anne, who recommends befriending the women who might initially intimidate you. Those women who seem to have it so "together" all the time? The women who you catch yourself feeling envious of? Don't hate them, get to know them.

We achieve our goals faster when we strive together, anyway, so I'm all about flipping the script from competition to collaboration and befriending the badass women I've met along the way. But

I'll be the first to admit it: that mental backbend ain't easy! Have you ever rage-quit Instagram because watching someone else's glow-up is just too irritating to bear? I know you know what I'm talking about . . .

When I first started Bossed Up, I felt envious at every turn. Social media makes it easier than ever to get caught in the comparison trap, and I never thought I'd measure up to the other boss ladies I admired. But jealousy hijacks your heart and holds you hostage from your own success. The more I focused on what other people were up to in their businesses, the less I was focused on my own. When I found myself feeling bitter over someone else's achievement, there was less love in my heart for everyone else— me included.

When I started actively reaching out and surrounding myself with those I admired, celebrating their successes became easier because I started to feel like we were part of a squad that strives together and thrives together. When they had great opportunities come their way, they'd pass them along and lift me up with them. I made sure to bring fellow boss ladies along for the ride whenever I could, too. For instance, when Bossed Up was hired by a middle school to produce a custom Bossed Up Bootcamp for seventh-grade girls and their moms, I included some members of our team of certified Bossed Up trainers in the bid. Together, we partnered to ensure the smooth delivery of a custom program presented by trainers who reflected a diverse array of industries and backgrounds. And, yes, I've benefited from being included in my peers' projects as well. It seems the more successful your friends become, the more success comes *your* way, too.

Instead of feeling envious, we were all cheering for each other. Instead of feeling less than, I felt proud to support our squad. But it takes building real, authentic relationships with people you admire to really bridge that gap. Once I saw that we were all on our own journey of figuring it out, that we were all working with different strengths and challenges, I realized that most of us are in the same boat, after all.

Shine theory works right alongside mirror theory in an interesting way:

Mirror theory is all about how we can provide *internal reinforcement* to one another as we shape our sense of self and cultivate the boss identity we need to be our most courageous selves. It's focused on being there for each other in the hard times, with our abiding belief in one another's ability to persevere and rise up.

Shine theory is all about how we can provide that *external reinforcement* and really showcase and celebrate one another's successes. It's about not dropping off the map in the good times—and feeling a genuine happiness for one another's triumphs (which often means fighting off the totally understandable temptation of succumbing to jealousy).

None of us achieves greatness in total isolation. We need inspiration and reinforcement from people we trust and admire in the good times *and* the hard times. And we need to move beyond the idea that a single magical mentor is sufficient.

More Than a Mentor

Sometime in the past decade or two, all the college guidance counselors and career coaches seem to have lost their damn minds with mentor mania. You know the drill: everyone's supposed to have a mentor—some elusive sage who is accomplished and important and yet also somehow has the time to

take you under his or her wing and show you the secrets of career success.

The calls to action make for hot headlines. We need more
women mentoring women! We need more men mentoring women!
We need more mentoring programs! No—we need more online
mentoring algorithms!

Enough. Mentorship is the most overpromised, underdeliv-
ered "secret to success" out there.

Now, don't get me wrong, I have benefited greatly from the advice and wisdom of older friends and business associates, including my favorite college professor, who continues to make the effort
to keep in touch even ten years postgraduation.

But the term "mentorship" brings such unnecessary—and I
would argue harmful—formality to the relationship. The real secret is in building authentic, productive relationships, ideally with
mutual benefit. As Sandberg notes in *Lean In,* being asked, "Will
you be my mentor?" is awkward at best and annoying at worst.
Would you walk up to someone in high school and say, "Will you
be my friend?" It's not exactly a relationship fire starter.

Another beef I have with mentorship? Mentors are just as
likely to perpetuate bias as any other imperfect human being.[6] Our
implicit biases lead us to want to mentor people who remind us
of our younger selves. So what do you think that means for our
white, male-dominated world? Making mentor matters worse,
when women who've been chronically underpaid are the only ones
advising younger women on their salary expectations, systemic
biases persist. Despite the best of intentions, the emphasis on mentorship sets us up to perpetuate injustices.

"But Emilie, that's why we have formal mentorship programs!"
you might be thinking. "They do something to eliminate bias,

right?" Yes, they do. And they also provide the oh-so-pleasant experience of career speed-dating. You get the fun of being set up on a blind date to talk about career interests, and some poor mentorship program manager has to hear from disgruntled parties on both sides and try to mediate a hundred different formally constructed relationships at once. Oof.

And can we acknowledge just how much pressure this mentorship obsession puts on *one* relationship? If you're lucky enough to find yourself with a mentor you get along with, that person can't be counted on to answer all your tough career questions, especially because (spoiler alert!) your mentor is likely not a career expert him- or herself! Of course industry expertise is essential, but putting all our eggs in one or two mentors' baskets just doesn't seem like a sound strategy to me.

Before you bust out the torches and pitchforks, hear me out: I'm not saying that mentor-like relationships are not important—they very much are. I just think it's time to retire the formal misnomer and see the value in having a whole *community* of people to turn to when you need the courage and support to boss up.

In the same way that diversity helps corporate boards make better decisions, a healthy variety of folks in your community will make *you* better.[7] It's not just about having older, successful mentors. How about those lateral, peer-to-peer relationships with people who, just like you, are figuring it out? We need relationships that are vertical and horizontal, with people younger and older, across industries and geographies, and of any gender. Beyond our professional network, we need loved ones—friends, romantic partners, and family—who we can turn to and ask for help, whether it's a pick-me-up text or a literal pick-me-up-off-the-floor kinda hug.

Without Bossed Up's incredible community of expert trainers—my amazing peers—we would never have the impact we've had thus far. Without my board of advisors, Bossed Up wouldn't have emerged from that postlaunch rocky patch. And without the unwavering love and support of my main squeeze, who saw in me a woman a hundred times stronger than I knew I could be, I honestly wouldn't be writing these words today.

You need a squad. A crew to roll with. A diverse **community of courage** you can go to with your audacious goals *and* the challenges that make you feel most vulnerable.

SPOTLIGHT

"I thought I was too shy to grow my network."

LeAndria is a naturally soft-spoken, reserved Southern belle. Raised in South Carolina, she found the strength to speak up and assert herself in a whole new way through Bossed Up, and she wanted to help us reach even more women. So, after attending Bossed Up Bootcamp, LeAndria stepped up to become our DC AmBOSSador—a volunteer community-organizing role in our founding city, where she would help host free networking events for women to get to know the Bossed Up community.

At the start of our AmBOSSador program, LeAndria worked with me to develop her "story of self" as a means to introduce herself, explain her motivations and credentials, and win over the trust and support of anyone she might speak with.

She tapped into why she felt so strongly about our mission and was able to clearly articulate her passion to anyone new.

She used her story of self to reach out and connect over coffee with like-minded organizers behind local brands and small businesses she might partner with to host events. She organized sip 'n shop parties at local boutiques, happy hours with fellow feminist organizations, and even a tea party at a local business. Over time, the groundwork LeAndria laid and the relationships she nurtured resulted in her events regularly garnering RSVPs in the hundreds.

"I was making a positive impact and making a name for myself," said LeAndria, who admitted she never set out to grow her personal reach.

As she became more comfortable with public speaking, bringing people together, and pulling off events where anyone could come in and feel like a part of the community, her reputation grew, too. At events, LeAndria would share a few words about herself and our community, and women would come up and introduce themselves, often offering plans to meet and talk further one-on-one.

"I used to think I was too shy to 'build my brand,' whatever that means," LeAndria recounted. "But I reframed it as problem solving. The AmBOSSador role was my way of paying it forward on the enriching Bossed Up experience I had, and in doing so I actually grew my skill set even more."

After her yearlong tenure as AmBOSSador was up, LeAndria was still hooked on growing her community impact, so she sought out the opportunity to lead a group of women in her industry. As the leader of a DC Women in Technology group,

LeAndria grew the local chapter from eighty to three hundred in one year and, once again, saw her own reputation expand along with it.

While facilitating connection among other women in her world of technology consulting, LeAndria found herself stagnating at what was once an exciting job. She'd just been passed over for a promotion after three years serving in the same role and was craving growth, challenge, and change. She realized the network she'd cultivated could serve as an immense resource to her at this critical time and started exploring new opportunities through her many connections.

She followed a lead that one of her newfound friends had mentioned over a cocktail and soon found herself interviewing. Ultimately, she received an offer to step up in the first handful of consultants in the DC office of a new technology firm that was expanding into the city, and it included the opportunity to lead the shaping of the program itself. The offer was for more money than she'd ever been paid, and she still managed to negotiate the deal further, landing at a 43 percent compensation bump from her last job.

"I'm excited to develop my business acumen," said LeAndria, who's thrilled to be starting in this new capacity. "Community building and becoming more comfortable as a speaker definitely helped me craft my public persona—and that was a big piece in my strategy for advancing my career."

One Relationship at a Time

So how do you make all this happen? One relationship at a time. I'm a community organizer at my core, and, let me tell you, relationships are the building blocks of every successful cause, campaign, and movement.

Think of your life as your cause, your career as your campaign, and build yourself a community of courage, boss! Here's how I like to break the process down:

1. Identify What You Want to Learn—Not Who You Want to Know

When you don't yet know the people who can open doors for you and impart the right wisdom at just the right moment, it can be difficult to know where to turn. Instead, focus on what you need to learn to make your vision a reality. From there, think about where you might find folks who might know more about that. Go to where those people might be (think free meetups, happy hours, industry events, online forums), and don't forget to ask your friends and colleagues already in your network for their recommendations. Sometimes that means you have to fly solo at events, which I realize can be a scary experience, especially for my introvert bosses out there. But showing up is what you do when you really love someone, so give yourself and your vision the same courtesy.

2. Ask to Ask

Once you've identified someone you think might be helpful in your pursuits, ask for a conversation first. A few years back, I was looking for a developer to assist with my WordPress-hosted website, and I really wanted to work with women developers who were local. To start this process, I rolled up to a WordPress Meetup night in DC. At that meetup, I met a few different people I wanted to get to know further to explore an opportunity for collaboration and get their insight on some big website questions I was wrestling with. I didn't immediately dive into my big website conundrums right then and there at the meetup, before we'd had a chance to get to know each other. Instead, I shared what I was doing, alluded to my overarching goals for improving my site, and asked whether they'd be willing to grab a coffee later that week to see whether we might be of help to one another.

Giving folks a sense of what you'd like to learn about and how you might be of assistance to them (even if the two are totally unrelated) is a great way to ask for a phone call or meeting. Be sure to send a succinct email the next day with a few proposed meeting times for their consideration.

3. Focus on the Why

Once you've landed the one-on-one meeting, focus on sharing *why* you're doing what you're doing and learn more about the other person's motivations as well. Let's say you're looking for a job in higher education and having meetings with a few administrators at universities in your area. Don't just tell that person about your achievements and credentials, tell a story that illustrates why you care. Why are you called to teaching? Why are you making a job transition now?

In the same way, ask about their origin stories. How did they end up where they are today? What choices did they make along the way and, importantly, *why?* "Why" questions are so critical because they help to articulate your values. The choices we make that steer our lives in one direction or another are reflections of our core values, and they're a gateway into understanding a person and building an authentic relationship.

4. Aim for the Magic X

The magic X is the intersection between your shared values and diverse resources. Once you've both shared the *why* behind the "what you do" and hopefully uncovered some of the values that you two share, the next step is to identify what unique resources you both bring to the table that can help further your goals.

What do you have to share? Time? Energy? Resources? Connections? People power?

And what do you need to move forward? Job leads? Negotiation help? A resume review? Connections?

What resources does the person you're meeting with have that you lack? Odds are, you've already done a good deal of thinking about this before asking your contact to meet, but now's the time to remain flexible and open to uncovering new resources through conversation that you may not have learned about by stalking him or her on LinkedIn.

5. Make a Clear Ask

Once you've identified what resources you both bring to the table, ask for the specific help you need and want. By this point in the conversation, you've already explained your motivations and hopefully bonded with the person about your shared values. So now is the time to offer your new amiga an opportunity to take concrete action on those shared values: Will you introduce me to the hiring managers at your company? Will you listen to my demo reel and provide me with your feedback? Can you proofread my resume? Will you cohost this event with me? Will you commit to bringing in five of your friends to our program? Will you build/write/do this thing with me?

If the answer is yes or maybe, get specific about when, where, and how you propose moving forward.

If the answer is in the negative, ask an open-ended question for suggestions as to how to proceed. You'd be surprised how many folks will offer another way they can help or advise you to move forward.

Then—and this is key—offer up your own resources or assistance in helping that person in return in furthering some of his or her goals or objectives you uncovered through your conversation. If you can't think of anything concrete at the moment, you can always say something like, "Please let me know if I can ever be of assistance to you, as well." Wrap things up with gratitude and paint a clear picture of what is to come next.

Remember, making a clear, solid ask isn't something to be sheepish about. It is a courtesy to the person who's spending his or her time to try to be of assistance to you. Make it easy for that person to help by making a succinct, specific request!

6. Follow Up

No matter how flawless your one-on-one meeting game is, the real magic is in the follow-up.

Send a timely (within twenty-four hours) email thanking your contact again for his or her time and delivering on any of what you promised you'd send along. Set clear expectations of how you'd like to move forward and send any materials needed to do so.

Remember, this is just the start of an ongoing relationship. Keep in touch with these contacts even after they're done helping you along your way. If you hit it off, stay on each other's radars by inviting them to events you're heading to, sharing articles you think they'd find interesting, and dropping them a casual note of appreciation when you're thinking about them.

Making one-on-one meetings a priority can be an incredibly effective strategy for growing your community and advancing all kinds of goals you're pursuing—especially when it comes to finding your next job opportunity.

By building authentic, reciprocal relationships, you'll ensure that you're growing your community, your power, and your knowledge base alongside people who share your values and want to see you succeed as much as you're cheering them on in return.

SPOTLIGHT

"You have the power to make your own opportunity."

Jessica was laid off from a job she loathed in June. Although it was hard to be upset about the loss, she knew that if she didn't take an assertive role in making her next move, she was going to wind up having to take another dead-end job.

That's why Jessica devoted her summer to growing her community in a deliberate and strategic way, with the ultimate goal of finding the job that was right for her—not making *her-self* "right" for just any job.

As a passionate advocate fighting on behalf of underserved communities in the nonprofit sector for years, Jessica knew that she wanted a position in service of others and recognized that her skills and experience were valuable assets.

Instead of focusing on searching and applying for jobs on-line, Jessica initiated a series of casual conversations with key stakeholders she respected. She reached out to executive di-rectors at local charities and nonprofits she admired and asked them to coffee. One by one, they swapped stories and explored their commonalities. Each meeting ended with a series of refer-rals to other key players for Jessica to contact.

"Getting into a job interview cold can be really hard now-adays," said Jessica. "There's just so much competition and tal-ent out there. So having these one-on-one meetings felt like more of a conversation than a formal process. They helped me explore what I was interested in and really allowed me to be myself."

Sometimes, Jessica realized, you don't need a single, long-term mentor—you need a short-term squad to help you achieve a singular goal.

"I relied on one-on-one meetings because I know it's even harder for me to get through the doors of big institutions as a woman of color," Jessica told me. "I reached out to many women of color whose careers inspired me, who served as role models for me, and it was so important for me to have that kind of crew to lean on throughout this process."

By reaching out with clear, concise emails that made it easy for these VIPs to help, Jessica grew her community and made her skills and availability known. She was always transparent in her outreach, making clear what her goals were and what kinds of advice and feedback she was looking for.

"You have to be honest," she said, "because if not you can come across as misleading and just using someone for your own gain. Whenever there's anything I can do in return, even if it's just buying their coffee, I'm always looking to reciprocate."

She admits, however, as a self-proclaimed introvert, reaching out and growing her community in this way did not come easily to her. But, because she knew how critically important this strategy was for her long-term career success, Jessica was willing to step outside her comfort zone and initiate these meetings.

"You have to just do it," she told me, "as awkward or uncomfortable as it might feel. For me, the hardest part was sending that initial outreach email, but, after every conversation I had, I so appreciated the fact that I'd done it. At the end, I'd ask for their support in helping me reach out to at least one other person they know who I should be connecting with, too. That made it easier to keep going."

After two months of consistent outreach and one-on-one meetings, Jessica found the organization and role for her, formally applied, and received an offer higher than she anticipated. Even though she was pleased with the initial salary offered, she decided to flex her negotiation muscles and counteroffered with a 5 percent increase that was accepted by her new boss.

Jessica started her new job shortly after Labor Day in a challenging but rewarding new position to help decrease the risk of HIV and STDs among young women in her community by promoting self-efficacy through safe-sex education. During her tenure there, she went back to school part-time, earning both her MSW and MPH degrees at Boston University, and then relied on her community once again to pivot into an even bigger role in data analysis and quality assessments of programming at a national nonprofit serving thousands more.

"By laying that groundwork, I ended up surrounding myself with this community of women—especially women of color—who lift each other up," said Jessica. "And, for anyone who's ever felt excluded from the mainstream, it's so important to know that you have the power to make your own opportunity, too."

You, too, can cultivate meaningful relationships one at a time by being *of value* to people and asking for their support in return. And hey, if this sounds transactional, that's because it is! Who says there's anything inherently wrong with that? Of course you don't need to swap favors with every friend, colleague, and family member in your life, but, at the end of the day, isn't showing up for each other what friends do?

Admittedly, making new friends gets harder as we get older.[8] Priorities shift, roles change, and geographic proximity to pals is harder to come by. Despite the hyper-connected nature of our digital world, we're experiencing what some public health officials call a loneliness "epidemic."[9] Putting in effort to stay truly connected to your community is not only a smart move for your career but also critical to your mental health and happiness.

It's up to each of us to consider maintaining our relationships not just as a nice-to-have luxury but a core component of a sustainable life. Think back to Maslow's hierarchy of needs: a sense of belonging is the third level of that foundation, just above food, water, and a sense of safety. You *must* protect your happiness like it's your job—and that means assertively eliminating the toxic, draining people in your life and doing the vulnerable, challenging work of maintaining healthy relationships. After all, when you are the boss of your life, you get to hire, fire, and promote accordingly.

You are worthy of love and belonging, boss. You are worthy of people in your life who lift you up, cheer you on, and believe in your audacious ambitions. You are worthy of people who care for you, just as you aim to care for them. And you are worthy of the time, energy, and effort it takes to build up that kind of a community around you.

Do More Together

We know having a community of support matters—both for our personal sustainability and professional success. Like so much of what goes into getting bossed up, it's not only the right *moral* thing to do for ourselves, but it's also the *most strategic* way forward.

Striving alongside a community of courage can make a big difference in terms of actually making those goals of yours a reality. In one study, participants were asked to share a goal they wanted to achieve over a four-week period.[10] Researchers found that participants who shared their goals and checked in with an accountability partner weekly accomplished significantly more than others who simply wrote down their goals or broke them down into action steps. The findings also showed support for the role of public commitment: those who sent their commitments to a friend at the start of the study accomplished significantly more as well.

The power of communal accountability is especially important for those of us who identify as "obligers," as author Gretchen Rubin calls them. In her book exploring habit formation, *Better Than Before,* Rubin introduces "the four tendencies," a series of categories people seem to fall into that shape our relationship with habits. Rubin describes obligers as follows:

> Obligers meet outer expectations, but struggle to meet inner expectations. They're motivated by *external accountability;* they wake up and think, "What *must* I do today?" Because obligers excel at meeting external demands and deadlines, and go to great lengths to meet their responsibilities, they make terrific colleagues, family members, and friends . . .
>
> Behavior that obligers sometimes attribute to *self-sacrifice—* "Why do I always make time for other people's priorities at the expense of my own priorities?"—is often better explained as *need for accountability.*
>
> The weight of outer expectations can make obligers susceptible to burnout, because they have trouble telling people "no." An obliger explained, "I drop everything to proofread my colleagues' reports, but I'm terrible about making time to finish my own reports."
>
> For them, the key is external accountability.[11]

Sound familiar? Although being an obliger might make you a great colleague, too much of this self-sacrifice amounts to the martyrdom mindset! The good news is, an accountability community can help folks who identify as obligers enormously.

It's part of the reason why the Bossed Up online community is such a powerful space. It's where women come together to share their goals, ask for help, share resources, and check in on their progress. A member of our group recently called it "the best place on Facebook," and it's also totally free, so get on over to BossedUp .com to join us there if you haven't already.

The amazing thing about having a system of support where you can be *real* and actually share your successes *and* stumbles is that having an accountability buddy can help you bounce back when you stumble, too.[12] There's a fascinating phenomenon in the long-term goal attainment research called **coindulgence** that has been shown to help us experience less guilt, get back on track faster, and foster stronger social bonds along the way. Researchers studied the behaviors of people who were trying to make progress on goals related to money, food, or time management. When people made decisions in small groups or with another person, their choice *alignment* was a critical factor. When they both abstained from a serious temptation (and passed on a pricey, high-calorie, or time-wasting indulgence), they strengthened their friendship and felt good about making progress on their goals together. "We did it! We're so good!"

But, to the researchers' surprise, when participants did choose to indulge a little—and satisfy their short-term desires by "cheating" on their long-term goals—the partners "found friendship through partnering in crime by both indulging." It's that friendship-fostering feeling of "Oooooh, we're so bad!" What really shocked researchers was that participants actually felt better and experienced less guilt when they had "a partner in crime" to share in their indulgence. They stayed out of self-loathing and seemed to get back on track in pursuit of their goals faster.

Even if you're taking two steps forward and one step backward on your goals, if you take that step back *with someone,* you're more likely to bond with your partner, get back on track faster, and experience less guilt. So, instead of secretly sneaking that cookie after your healthy lunch, have one with a friend, and you're less likely to sink into that productivity-killing shame spiral. Instead of procrastinating on Facebook, alone in the office, give yourself a break to FaceTime with a family member, and you'll return more refreshed and ready to finish the task at hand.

Going it alone is neither pleasant nor pragmatic. It serves us all better to team up—and lift each other up as we go. You don't get there faster by going solo. In most cases, we'll achieve more (and have a better time doing it) together. Keep striving and keep thriving with a community of courage beside you—especially when the going gets tough.

If a former "lone wolf" like me can do it, so can you. In fact, it's quite likely that this book wouldn't be written without me taking some of my own advice on this front. As I finalized my manuscript this very moment, I asked my college bestie for her support and accountability. It just so happens that we're both in the midst of planning our weddings, which are happening about a month apart this year and are delightfully fun distractions when we'd rather be finalizing bachelorette party details than doing real work. While I'm trying to finish writing this book, she's trying to finish her PhD dissertation, a comparably enormous undertaking.

So, each morning for the past few weeks, ever since we decided to be accountability buddies for each other, I've woken up with a text message from her. She lives on the East Coast and starts her days a few hours before I do from my new digs in Denver, and it's wonderful to see words of encouragement from her and her concrete, measurable writing goals for the day. It forces me to sit down and clarify (if I hadn't already the day before) what my objectives are for the day ahead and report in to her. Then, throughout the day when we're feeling distracted and stuck or triumphant and productive, we report in to one another. At the end of the day, no matter how things go, we try to always send a final status update, review all the progress we made, and cheer each other on. Needless to say, we use many, many encouraging emojis to send each other props from afar.

The best part? It makes us feel good (and not guilty!) about all the time we spend talking bridal details with one another, too, because we know that we're not just procrastinating and distracting ourselves from the work at hand, because we're so accountable to one another on our work progress, too.

Just knowing that I have someone so supportive to check in with has rapidly improved my productivity, but the biggest difference is actually in my mindset. Writing, like many professional pursuits, can feel like a lonely endeavor at times (even though I get to interview so many rad women for their spotlight features in this book!). When it's just me in my own head, the blinking cursor on the page in front of me can be daunting. I second-guess myself, sentence by sentence. I can fall into negative self-talk just like anyone might, thinking that what I'm doing makes no sense or won't have the impact I intend. In isolation, it's hard to pump yourself up. It's hard to be your own hype woman.

We all need someone to hold up the mirror for us at times and reflect back a more capable and courageous version of ourselves than we think is possible. My college bestie is holding that mirror up for me now, and I'm grateful to be able to reciprocate, especially on those hard days. We all have the power to reach out, to assertively ask for the support we need, and to give back as best we can. That's what my personal community of courage is all about, and I'd love to welcome you with open arms into our Bossed Up community, too. There, anyone who's been going it alone can find women committed to lifting as they climb.

Partners and Professional Success

Thus far we've talked a lot about building your community of courage through professional networking and leaning on friends. And there's a reason for that: I don't think any woman needs a romantic partner in her life in order to strive for sustainable success. You're a whole person already. It's incumbent upon all of us to build a squad of loved ones around us, but that by no means requires finding this one special person who's supposed to meet your every need for the rest of your life.

But, as a marriage skeptic on the cusp of diving into the institution myself, I would be remiss to not acknowledge the overlap between our romantic and professional lives. After all, at every Bossed Up Bootcamp, we feature a licensed therapist who focuses on love and relationships, and it's always one of the most interesting parts of the weekend. With a room full of women who are navigating career crossroads and looking to level up in their lives, we have a *lot* to say when it comes to romantic partners and the impact they have on our career choices.

This is a topic I've long wrestled with. While I was in the midst of one of my many troubled relationships in college (he was a serial cheater, and my sense of self-worth was fragile enough to go back to him again and again), I wrote a long paper in a philosophy class on feminist political theory. My topic? Debating whether romantic love and gender equality could be reconciled. How can you love someone, *unconditionally,* as we're taught to think of love, and yet also demand equality in your relationship and household?

You can't, I finally concluded, after getting a monthlong extension on the paper and falling into an oh-so-collegiate existential crisis. As depressing as the paper was, I'm glad to say it helped me recognize the bogus relationship I was in at the time, and I moved on from it shortly thereafter. I wasn't out of the woods just yet (there were *many* more messed-up relationships ahead for me), but, hey, I was iterating.

This is a troubling topic for me because the research on romance and feminism is so full of contradictions and conundrums for women with ambition and a desire for love in our lives (a.k.a. all of us). In a recent business school study, for instance, researchers found that single women reported lower levels of career ambition (lower desired pay, lower tolerance of work travel) when they were required to share their goals publicly among their peers.[13] When women knew that their responses would be seen only by a career counselor, single women and attached women answered similarly—and with higher self-reported ambitions. Researchers concluded that part of what caused the single women to aim lower when sharing their goals with their classmates was the fear of reducing their appeal in the "marriage marketplace." They know, like I did, that although women's ambition is all the rage in our politically correct culture, being *too* into your career goals is still a boner kill.[14]

These studies, like much of the research on gender and romantic love, was unfortunately limited to cis, heterosexual people, and I'm quite confident that results would be different in LGBTQ+ communities, where being forthright with your romantic *and* career preferences is more par for the course.

But as far as heterosexual pairings go, we're living through some awkward times when it comes to being ambitious and seeking a romantic partner. For starters, we have that evidence that single women tend to downplay their ambitions when men are around, which must set the stage for future frustration in relationships, no? And then there's evidence that those women are being cautious for a reason: although men *say* they admire intelligence and ambition in their desired female partners, up close they actually feel emasculated, inferior, and turned off.[15]

Despite all the (depressing AF) evidence, I'm still an unbridled optimist when it comes to partners and professional ambitions. In part it's my own lucky experience that's the source of my sunshiny bias on this, and it's partly due to a few bright spots in the data. First, it's significant to note that people in "high-quality" relationships have higher levels of happiness and health than those who are in the *wrong* relationship, which can be incredibly destructive to one's health.[16] And for those who find themselves in a relationship gone south, it's more socially acceptable than ever for women to GTFO. Being single, time and again, is found to be better for your health and happiness by far than being in a "low-quality" relationship.

Furthermore, women in healthy relationships report higher levels of risk tolerance professionally. It's almost as though when you're launching your career with a solid relationship as your foundation, you're willing to aim higher, whether that means starting that business, going for that big career change, or running for office. Knowing that someone's got your back (emotionally, financially, or otherwise) makes women more willing to take big leaps.

That certainly rings true to my experience, and it's a big part of the reason I've decided to walk down the aisle with Brad (the boo) later this year. When I met him, more than six years ago now, I was playing volleyball on the beach courts down on the National

Mall, hidden away from tourists behind the Lincoln Memorial on the bank of the Potomac. Getting back into my college sport was part of my healing process when recovering from burnout and my former, truly toxic relationship. I was rediscovering my physical strength and, with it, my mental fortitude, too. And I was *playing* again. Suddenly life didn't feel so damn serious all the time, and I had a renewed sense of gratitude for every moment I had to spend on this planet. Having turned the page on what was the darkest chapter in my life to date, I was committed to making this next phase a lot lighter.

So, as I was crushing it in a domain where I felt very confident, I stumbled into Brad, standing on the sidelines having just finished a game himself. As I was begrudgingly untying Teddy (the dog) from the post where he was tied up in the shade so I could run to the restroom a hundred yards away, I looked up and saw Brad standing there, offering to watch him for me instead. We exchanged maybe five words, and that was it. "Thanks!" I yelled over my shoulder, as I jogged back onto court for my next match.

I kept playing volleyball, and he kept showing up. His game was a little rough around the edges, but he had impressive hustle (his skills as the number one tennis player on his college team translated well to the volleyball court). Over the next few weeks we would exchange numbers and casually start going to grab a bite to eat after daylong volleyball extravaganzas. Eventually, I'd get a quick smooch in the car before dropping him off at his place afterward. By the end of the summer, we entered a beach volleyball tournament together as teammates, and we haven't stopped acting that way since.

There's this cliché quote about daring greatly by Henry David Thoreau that goes, "Proceed confidently in the direction of your dreams." I always thought that advice ended a little too abruptly. It should finish with, "and see who else is hanging out there!" That's what made the difference for me: when I started actively pursuing the life I wanted, unafraid of what people would think, unconcerned with being "the best," and actually stopped hustling 24/7 to *do me* for a change, I ran into the kind of people who were into that, too, including Brad.

Since then, we've both navigated huge career shifts. Brad quit his stable, steady architecture job to start his own digital fabrication shop in a garage right around the time I quit my job to start Bossed Up. We leveraged that first entrepreneurial venture of his into landing his dream job at a high-end fabrication shop in Denver, once we decided together that the Rocky Mountains were calling our names. Last year we bought and renovated a house in Denver together, and, as I write this, we're less than two months out from our wedding day.

There's a controversial quote from Sheryl Sandberg's *Lean In* that comes to mind when it comes to marriage. She said, "The most important career decision you'll make is who you marry," a bold statement from a woman who could never have predicted that she would lose her husband to an untimely death just a few short years later. I certainly don't believe you have to "put a ring on it" to find support in a committed partner, and I happen to know many a single lady whose career is doing just dandy, thank you very much. But when it comes to navigating this game called life, I feel unstoppable as a member of this particular duo. And, hell, we're not even dealing with the realities of doling out childcare duties just yet (a universal challenge for any couple striving to maintain a gender-equitable partnership).

There's a hidden privilege to having a life partner that I don't think we talk about often enough, too. This isn't to say my single friends aren't equally capable, but, as one of them put it to me, "There's nobody around to let the cable guy in when I'm at work." Or cable gal, I suppose. But the point is, it's harder to juggle all those roles and obligations in our lives unless we can tag-team with a wingman or wingwoman.

At every Bossed Up Bootcamp, we break down how we're thinking about and incorporating healthy love (romantic, platonic, and otherwise) into our lives, because those relationships absolutely do bleed over into our careers. I'm often struck by how many of our ambitious attendees—who are happy to rattle off the audacious goals they have for their careers—are sheepish when it comes to articulating what they want out of love. It's like we've been told not to ask for what we really want in our relationships. Or as if saying it out loud might jinx our chances. Or maybe, just maybe, so many of us carry with us the wounds we suffered from past experiences and know only what we *don't want* in our lives, and lose sight of what we would *love* in our love lives.

Either way, at the end of the day, it's hard to be goal oriented in this arena because it's not all on us, right? We can't predict what someone else is going to do or want, how he or she might evolve, or what might change. But hold up—isn't that true about all our other goals, too? Our careers? Our health? See, those excuses don't hold up for me anymore. I think it's time for us to give ourselves permission to explore and articulate what we really want out of our love lives, especially in terms of how they relate to our professional ambitions. And, yes, even if what you want pushes back on the feminist "mainstream." Wanting a committed, loving relationship doesn't make you some kind of traditionalist or bad feminist—nor does taking action to make that a priority in your life.

I'm not saying that anyone should pursue a marriage or relationship just for the perks of having someone around to let the cable guy (or gal!) in, though. Like I mentioned, being in an unhealthy relationship will bum you out *way* more than being on your own. You're already a whole person, you don't need someone to complete you. And maybe you're perfectly happy staying single. But if you *do* crave a companion, if you want a real partner in crime, give yourself permission to make that a goal you're pursuing just like any other ambition. Break it into subgoals. Set yourself up with an accountability partner. Be deliberate about seeking out what you want—because you're worth the effort. Even though dating is kind of the worst (and I am *no* dating expert myself), the pursuit of deep, intimate connection deserves to be a priority in your life. And you know what? Your career won't suffer because of it, your career will be fine.

We've been told for far too long that "work-life balance," whatever the hell that is, is a challenge that women will face and women will have to deal with. But it's not on us alone to figure this out. In fact, it all depends on who we're negotiating that balance with. Who's on your team? Who's part of your support system? And, importantly, how does your employer feel about personal lives and families?

For, my fellow Americans, we still live in a country whose government has done very little to make those negotiations easier. Without uniform legislation on parental leave rights, affordable childcare reform, or support in caring for aging parents, it's the wild, wild West out here. Whether it's negotiating for the benefits you need from your employer or what you need from your partner to make it work, we have to be clear on our vision for the life we want for ourselves and have the audacity to be assertive in making it a reality. As the boss of your life, you get to negotiate those terms and conditions for yourself, with a community of courage that has your back.

Conclusion

You Have What You Need

Whoa, you made it to the end of my book! Amazing! Pat yourself on the back, boss, because you've already made *major* progress on getting bossed up yourself. It's my hope that within these pages, you've found some new tools to propel you forward with an unwavering belief in your ability to steer your career and life.

Because, listen, it's never been more important for women to sit in the driver's seat of our lives. Watching your life unfold before you, happen to you, from the passenger-side window is no longer an option.

We face enormous challenges ahead of us as a world—everything from wealth inequality to climate change to equal access to education to the unknown workforce consequences of AI. We need women at the helm solving these problems because, as Warren Buffet once put it, the problems we face will require "unlocking 100% of our human potential."[1]

And, although women's voices have always been a part of the chorus of people fighting for change, finally, it seems, the world is *listening* to women in a new way. The rise of #MeToo and #TimesUp, the historic numbers of women who ran for office in 2018, and the continued commitments to gender equality that we're seeing across corporate America leave me hopeful.

At the 2018 United State of Women Summit, I heard Michelle Obama share how she wants us women to seize this moment when our voices are finally being heard in a bold, assertive way:

> So many of us have gotten ourselves at the table, but we're still so grateful to *just be at the table* to really shake it up . . . and that's not a criticism, because for so many just getting to the table was so hard, right? And so you're just holding on. But now we have to take some risks for our girls, we have to be willing to lose a little bit of something. Just holding onto our seats at the table won't help our girls be all that they can be. And I think it's going to be on us as women to change that, but men have an important role to play as well.[2]

The way things have been done does *not* need to remain the way things are. But you gotta be willing to risk it, to put yourself out there, to be bold with your leadership, in order to push for progress. We can't get scared as we ascend in achieving our goals. We have to think about lifting as we climb: growing *our* power in order to leverage that power on behalf of those women and girls who come after us.

That's why I feel so strongly about women owning their power as the boss of their own careers and lives—as the main characters of our own come-up stories.

And yes, that's gonna take some work:

★ You must get out of the martyr mindset first and have the audacity to define what *you* want most out of your career and life.

★ You have to give yourself permission to dream big and articulate those dreams—not just when it comes to your career but in your personal life, too.

★ And you must be willing to assert yourself—even when it feels risky—in order to make progress on those dreams for yourself *and* others.

★ You have to be willing to be patient in your pursuits and treat yourself with compassion, self-care, and resilience through the process of realistic, strategic goal setting.

★ And, most critically, you must remember that, just because you're the boss, you don't have to go it alone.

It's not cute to celebrate the "hot mess" version of ourselves—which we've all been at one point or another. Helplessness is not a good look. No, we're *grown* women, as Beyoncé says. And not only do we know what we want, but we can proceed with the calm confidence that we're gonna get it, too. You have what you need, boss, now go get it.

Acknowledgments

Writing a book is an intimidating endeavor, and this particular book, which has been a work in progress for nearly four years, was no exception. Along the way, taking a bit of my own advice and drawing upon my personal community of courage made all the difference. Without the guidance, feedback, support, and encouragement from the following people, this book would remain unwritten.

First and foremost, I must thank my partner in crime, endless font of inspiration, and the man who always has more confidence in me than I do in myself, Brad Bolte. Brad was my first reader, and he left me thoughtful notes in every single chapter I wrote in their first (and most terrible) iteration, as I wrote them in real time. Brad, the devotion you've shown me in both your words of encouragement and practical assistance has set the gold standard for what I believe a true partnership should entail. So know that you've set that high bar for yourself, dude.

I must also thank my college bestie who's mentioned a few times throughout the book, Vanessa Merker. Vanessa, your accountability, empathy, and encouragement were instrumental in the completion of this manuscript. I consider myself fortunate to have such a witty, wise, and accomplished best friend—and now one with a proper PhD. Damn, girl!

Finally, without the endless love, support, and, frankly, inspiration provided by my incredible two parents, this book would not exist. Mom, the way you lead your life is awe inspiring to me, and I hope to follow in your footsteps and lead with love in everything I do. Dad, thank you for introducing me to Kendrick Lamar, and generally giving me my musical and cultural education. You're by far the coolest old white guy I've ever met.

Now to thank the professionals behind the absolute magic that went into making this book a million times better than I ever could have on my own. First to Colleen Lawrie, my talented editor, who I fell madly in love with when our first meeting in New York turned into the best, most never-ending professional date I've ever been on. Your smart advice, generous counsel, and early belief in my manuscript made this endeavor a reality. Thank you.

To Carrie Watterson, freelance copyeditor, and Brynn Warriner, senior project editor at Hachette, your skills made me a better writer and added a polish to this book that makes me proud to work with you and the entire Hachette Book Group team—especially since you badass bosses are also based here in Colorado!

To Ellie Nonemacher, the artist behind the graphics within these pages, as well as so much of the gorgeous art associated with Bossed Up online: thank you for your incredible creations that capture the essence of this community so well!

To my team at Bossed Up, including Emi Kamemoto, Kirby Verceles, and Jackie Butler: thank you for stepping up as leaders while I focused on bringing this creation to life. Your talents and devotion to our community made it possible for me to draw the boundaries I needed to write. I'm so proud of all we've created together.

Similarly, to the Bossed Up Bootcamp alums who shared their stories with me as part of this endeavor, Emma, Lauren, Jamie, Michelle, Maggie, Tiffany, Heather, Liz, Loryn, Helen, Jonelle, Eva, Sarah, LeAndria, and Jessica: thank you for being so courageous, candid, and generous with sharing your stories with me! You exemplify what it means to "lift as we climb" by sharing your own come-up stories as a means to inspire others. With your contributions, the lessons in this book become more within reach for so many of us who are inspired by how you've bossed up. I also want to thank another key Bossed Up community member, Maria Di Miceli, whose early feedback and support have been incredibly helpful as well.

Finally, I want to thank the entire Bossed Up community: the women in our Courage Community on Facebook, my podcast subscribers, and everyone who's ever used our LifeTracker Planners or attended Bossed Up Bootcamp in person. You inspire me to keep bossin' and do this work each and every day. You lift *me* when I'm down, and your stories of how you've stepped up to take the reins in your careers and lives give me life. Thank you for making what was once just a dream into my dream community, company, and job. It's a privilege to play a small role in helping you step up as the boss of your life.

Notes

Chapter 1: Combatting the Martyrdom Mindset

1. Brigid Schulte, "'The Second Shift' at 25: Q & A with Arlie Hochschild," She the People, *Washington Post*, August 6, 2014, www.washingtonpost.com/blogs/she-the-people/wp/2014/08/06/the-second-shift-at-25-q-a-with-arlie-hochschild/?utm_term=.f2210bfadffa.

2. Sharon Meers, "Women, Work and the 'Girl Scout Tax,'" At Work (blog), *Wall Street Journal*, October 29, 2013, https://blogs.wsj.com/atwork/2013/10/29/women-work-and-the-girl-scout-tax.

3. Liz O'Donnell, "The Crisis Facing America's Working Daughters," *Atlantic*, February 9, 2016, www.theatlantic.com/business/archive/2016/02/working-daughters-eldercare/459249.

4. Drew Desilver, "Access to Paid Family Leave Varies Widely Across Employers, Industries," Pew Research Center, March 23, 2017, www.pewresearch.org/fact-tank/2017/03/23/access-to-paid-family-leave-varies-widely-across-employers-industries.

5. Andrew J. Oswald, Eugenio Proto, and Daniel Sgroi, "Happiness and Productivity," *Journal of Labor Economics* 33, no. 4 (2015): 789–822, https://wrap.warwick.ac.uk/63228/7/WRAP_Oswald_681096.pdf.

6. Josh Mitchell, "Weak Productivity, Rising Wages Putting Pressure on U.S. Companies," *Wall Street Journal*, June 7, 2016, www.wsj.com/articles/u-s-productivity-fell-0-6-in-first-quarter-1465302710.

7. Jordan Weissmann, "Americans, Ever Hateful of Leisure, Are More Likely to Work Nights and Weekends," *Slate*, September 11, 2014, www.slate.com/blogs/moneybox/2014/09/11/u_s_work_life_balance_americans_are_more_likely_to_work_nights_and_weekends.html.

8. US Travel Association, Project Time Off, May 23, 2017, https://projecttimeoff.com/reports/the-state-of-american-vacation-2017.

9. Anne-Marie Slaughter's *Unfinished Business* and Brigid Schulte's *Overwhelmed* are two excellent books that make this case very persuasively.

10. In case it's not obvious, Sheryl Sandberg's *Lean In* is the most well-known book that makes this case. Claire Shipman and Catty Kay also make a similar argument in their book, *The Confidence Code.*

11. Barack Obama, "*Glamour* Exclusive: President Barack Obama Says, 'This Is What a Feminist Looks Like,'" *Glamour,* August 4, 2016, www.glamour.com/story/glamour-exclusive-president-barack-obama -says-this-is-what-a-feminist-looks-like.

12. Board of Governors of the Federal Reserve System, *Report on the Economic Well-Being of U.S. Households in 2017,* May 2018, www .federalreserve.gov/publications/files/2017-report-economic-well-being -us-households-201805.pdf.

13. Kilolo Kijakazi and Heather McCulloch, "Building Women's Wealth Is Key to Economic Security," *Slate,* May 29, 2018, https:// slate.com/human-interest/2018/05/gender-inequality-closing-the -wealth-gap-is-critical-to-future-financial-security.html.

14. Jonathan C. Smith, "The New Psychology of Relaxation and Renewal," *Biofeedback* 35, no. 3 (Fall 2007): 85–89, https://pdfs.semantic scholar.org/b1c5/d4e15a179ed6c414447934256a8077bd2fa5.pdf.

15. Jessica Olien, "Loneliness Is Deadly," *Slate,* August 23, 2013, https://slate.com/technology/2013/08/dangers-of-loneliness-social -isolation-is-deadlier-than-obesity.html.

16. Nicholas Bakalar, "Longevity: Bonds of Friendship, Not Family, May Add Years," *New York Times,* June 28, 2005, www.nytimes .com/2005/06/28/health/longevity-bonds-of-friendship-not-family -may-add-years.html.

17. "Motherhood," Red Table Talk, Facebook, May 7, 2018, www .facebook.com/redtabletalk/videos/motherhood/560356131030533.

Chapter 2: Cultivating Your Boss Identity

1. Herminia Ibarra, Robin J. Ely, and Deborah M. Kolb, "Women Rising: The Unseen Barriers," *Harvard Business Review,* September 2013, https://hbr.org/2013/09/women-rising-the-unseen-barriers.

2. Jon Swaine, "Hillary Clinton Advises Women to Take Criticism 'Seriously but Not Personally,'" *Guardian,* February 13, 2014, www.theguardian .com/world/2014/feb/13/hillary-clinton-melinda-gates-women-criticism.

3. William Christeson et al., *Ready, Willing, and Unable to Serve* (Washington, DC: Mission: Readiness, 2009), http://cdn.missionreadiness.org/NATEE1109.pdf.

4. Victoria L Brescoll and Eric Luis Uhlmann, "Can an Angry Woman Get Ahead? Status Conferral, Gender, and Expression of Emotion in the Workplace," *Psychological Science* 19, no. 3 (2008): 268–275, http://gap.hks.harvard.edu/can-angry-woman-get-ahead-status-conferral-gender-and-expression-emotion-workplace.

5. Steven J. Spencer, Claude M. Steele, and Diane M. Quinn, "Stereotype Threat and Women's Math Performance," *Journal of Experimental Social Psychology* 35, no. 1 (January 1999): 4–28, www.sciencedirect.com/science/article/pii/S0022103198913737.

6. Andrea S. Kramer and Alton B. Harris, "Why Women Feel More Stress at Work," *Harvard Business Review*, August 4, 2016, https://hbr.org/2016/08/why-women-feel-more-stress-at-work.

7. Kramer and Harris, "Why Women Feel More Stress at Work."

8. "Women in S&P 500 Companies," Catalyst, October 3, 2018, www.catalyst.org/knowledge/women-sp-500-companies.

9. Valentina Zarya, "Why There Are No Black Women Running Fortune 500 Companies," *Fortune*, January 16, 2017, http://fortune.com/2017/01/16/black-women-fortune-500.

10. Kramer and Harris, "Why Women Feel More Stress at Work."

11. Peggy Noonan, *What I Saw at the Revolution: A Political Life in the Reagan Era* (New York: Random House, 1990), 179.

12. Jim Collins and Jerry I. Porras, *Built to Last: Successful Habits of Visionary Companies* (New York: Harper Business, 2011).

13. Jim Carrey, "Full Speech: Jim Carrey's Commencement Address at the 2014 MUM Graduation (EN, FR, ES, RU, GR, . . .)," YouTube video, posted by Maharishi University of Management, May 30, 2014, www.youtube.com/watch?v=V80-gPkpH6M.

14. Elizabeth Gilbert, *Big Magic: Creative Living Beyond Fear* (New York: Riverhead Books, 2015), 236.

Chapter 3: Progress over Perfection

1. Eric Ries, *The Lean Startup* (New York: Crown Business, 2011).

2. Stephen J. Dubner, "The Upside of Quitting," Freakonomics (podcast), September 30, 2011, http://freakonomics.com/podcast/new-freakonomics-radio-podcast-the-upside-of-quitting.

3. Jessica Bacal, *Mistakes I Made at Work: 25 Influential Women Reflect on What They Got Out of Getting It Wrong* (New York: Penguin, 2014), 191.

4. Carol Dweck, *Mindset: The New Psychology of Success* (New York: Random House, 2016).

5. Roy F. Baumeister, Kathleen D. Vohs, and Dianne M. Tice, "The Strength Model of Self-Control," *Current Directions in Psychological Science* 16, no. 6 (December 1, 2007): 351–355, https://journals.sagepub.com /doi/abs/10.1111/j.1467-8721.2007.00534.x.

6. Catrin Finkenauer, Asuman Buyukcan-Tetik, Roy F. Baumeister, Kim Schoemaker, Meike Bartels, and Kathleen D. Vohs, "Out of Control: Identifying the Role of Self-Control Strength in Family Violence," *Current Directions in Psychological Science* 24, no. 4 (August 12, 2015): 261–266, https://cdp.sagepub.com/content/24/4/261.abstract. Jeremy D. Mackey and Pamela L. Perrewé, "The AAA (Appraisals, Attributions, Adaptation) Model of Job Stress: The Critical Role of Self-Regulation," *Organizational Psychology Review* 4, no. 3 (March 14, 2014): 258–278, https://journals .sagepub.com/doi/abs/10.1177/2041386614525072.

7. Elizabeth Gilbert, "Perfectionism Is Just Fear in Really Good Shoes," October 3, 2014, www.elizabethgilbert.com/perfectionism -is-just-fear-in-really-good-shoes-dear-ones-enjoy-this-littl.

Chapter 4: Speak It, Be It

1. "Nicki Minaj—Bossing Up," YouTube video, posted by Kiana-BronxNy, January 14, 2011, www.youtube.com/watch?v=PzGZamtl RP0.

2. Marianne Cooper, "For Women Leaders, Likability and Success Hardly Go Hand-in-Hand," *Harvard Business Review*, April 30, 2013, https://hbr.org/2013/04/for-women-leaders-likability-a.

3. Sheryl Sandberg and Adam Grant, "Speaking While Female," *New York Times*, January 12, 2015, www.nytimes.com/2015/01/11 /opinion/sunday/speaking-while-female.html.

4. Marguerite Rigoglioso, "Researchers: How Women Can Succeed in the Workplace," *Insights*, March 1, 2011, www.gsb.stanford.edu/news /research/womencareerresearchbyoreilly.html.

5. "The Behavioral Science Guys: One Simple Skill to Curb Unconscious Gender Bias," YouTube video, posted by VitalSmarts Video, August 4, 2015, www.youtube.com/watch?v=SEHi4yauhu8.

6. Herminia Ibarra, Robin J. Ely, and Deborah M. Kolb, "Women Rising: The Unseen Barriers," *Harvard Business Review*, September 2013, https://hbr.org/2013/09/women-rising-the-unseen-barriers.

7. Sandberg and Grant, "Speaking While Female."

8. Juliet Eilperin, "How a White House Women's Office Strategy Went Viral," *Washington Post*, October 25, 2016, www.washingtonpost.com/news/powerpost/wp/2016/10/25/how-a-white-house-womens-office-strategy-went-viral/?utm_term=.2773fd10b639.

9. James R. Detert, Ethan R. Burris, and David A. Harrison, "Women Are Afraid to Speak Up? Really?," *Harvard Business Review*, June 1, 2010, https://hbr.org/2010/06/women-speak-up-less-than-men-really.

10. Ruchika Tulshyan, "Speaking Up as a Woman of Color at Work," *Forbes*, February 10, 2015, www.forbes.com/sites/ruchikatulshyan/2015/02/10/speaking-up-as-a-woman-of-color-at-work/#12bd64b69c1e.

11. "Phone Call," *Key and Peele*, January 31, 2012, www.cc.com/video-clips/qvrhhj/key-and-peele-phone-call.

12. Toby Harnden, "Caroline Kennedy Repeats 'You Know' 142 Times in Interview," *Telegraph*, December 29, 2008, www.telegraph.co.uk/news/worldnews/northamerica/usa/4015918/Caroline-Kennedy-repeats-you-know-142-times-in-interview.html.

13. Iain Thomas, "The Grand Distraction," June 19, 2012, www.iwrotethisforyou.me/2012/06/grand-distraction.html.

14. "If You Don't Have Anything Nice to Say, SAY IT IN ALL CAPS," act 2, "Freedom Fries," *This American Life*, January 23, 2015, 30:33, www.thisamericanlife.org/545/if-you-dont-have-anything-nice-to-say-say-it-in-all-caps/act-two.

15. Lesley Wolk, Nassima B. Abdelli-Beruh, and Dianne Slavin, "Habitual Use of Vocal Fry in Young Adult Female Speakers," *Journal of Voice* 26, no 3 (May 2012): e111–e116, www.jvoice.org/article/S0892-1997(11)00070-1/abstract.

16. Rindy C. Anderson, Casey A. Klofstad, William J. Mayew, and Mohan Venkatachalam, "Vocal Fry May Undermine the Success of Young Women in the Labor Market," *PLoS One*, 9, no. 5 (May 28, 2014): e97506, https://journals.plos.org/plosone/article?id=10.1371/journal.pone.0097506.

17. Faith Salie, "Burned Out on the Fry," *CBS Sunday Morning*, September 12, 2013, www.cbsnews.com/news/faith-salie-burned-out-on-the-fry.

18. Yana Skorobogatov, "What's Up with Upspeak?," *UC Berkeley Social Science Matrix*, September 21, 2015, https://matrix.berkeley.edu/research/whats-upspeak.

19. Jan Hoffman, "Overturning the Myth of Valley Girl Speak," *New York Times*, December 23, 2013, https://well.blogs.nytimes.com/2013/12/23/overturning-the-myth-of-valley-girl-speak.

20. Virginia Rutter, "Men and Women Use Uptalk Differently: A Study of Jeopardy!," *Sociological Images* (blog), *Society Pages*, December 28, 2013, https://thesocietypages.org/socimages/2013/12/28 /men-and-women-use-uptalk-differently-a-study-of-jeopardy.

21. Eben Harrell, "Wipe Away That Frown: Botox Makes You Happier," *Time*, March 31, 2009 http://content.time.com/time/health /article/0,8599,1888623,00.html.

22. Eva Ranehill et al., "Assessing the Robustness of Power Posing: No Effect on Hormones and Risk Tolerance in a Large Sample of Men and Women," *Psychological Science* 26, no. 5 (2015): 653–656, https:// journals.sagepub.com/doi/abs/10.1177/0956797614553946.

Chapter 5: Be a Goal Digger

1. Benjamin Franklin, *The Autobiography of Benjamin Franklin* (Kindle ed.).

2. Chip Heath and Dan Heath, *Switch: How to Change Things When Change Is Hard* (New York: Broadway Books, 2010), 7–8.

3. Heath and Heath, *Switch*, 8.

4. Heath and Heath, *Switch*, 82.

5. Lien B. Pham and Shelley E. Taylor, "From Thought to Action: Effects of Process- Versus Outcome-Based Mental Simulations on Performance," *Personality and Social Psychology Bulletin* 25, no. 2 (1999): 250–260, https://journals.sagepub.com/doi/abs/10.1177/014616729902 5002010.

6. Andrea Bonezzi, C. Miguel Brendl, and Matteo De Angelis, "Stuck in the Middle: The Psychophysics of Goal Pursuit," *Psychological Science* 22, no. 5 (April 7, 2011): 607–612, https://journals.sagepub.com /doi/abs/10.1177/0956797611404899.

7. Kelly Goldsmith and Anastasiya Pocheptsova Ghosh, unpublished study, 2018.

8. Teresa Amabile and Steven J. Kramer, "The Power of Small Wins," *Harvard Business Review*, May 2011, https://hbr.org/2011/05 /the-power-of-small-wins.

9. Katherine L. Milkman, Julia A. Minson, and Kevin G. M. Volpp, "Holding the Hunger Games Hostage at the Gym: An Evaluation of Temptation Bundling," *Management Science* 60, no. 2 (2013), https://pubsonline .informs.org/doi/abs/10.1287/mnsc.2013.1784.

10. Hengchen Dai, Katherine L. Milkman, and Jason Riis, "The Fresh Start Effect: Temporal Landmarks Motivate Aspirational Behavior,"

The Wharton School Research Paper No. 51, December 24, 2013, https://papers.ssrn.com/sol3/papers.cfm?abstract_id=2204126.

Chapter 6: Your Community of Courage

1. Marianne Cooper, "Why Women (Sometimes) Don't Help Other Women," *Atlantic,* June 23, 2016, www.theatlantic.com/business/archive/2016/06/queen-bee/488144.

2. Sheryl Sandberg and Adam Grant, "Sheryl Sandberg on the Myth of the Catty Woman," *New York Times,* June 23, 2016, www.nytimes.com/2016/06/23/opinion/sunday/sheryl-sandberg-on-the-myth-of-the-catty-woman.html.

3. Marianne Cooper, "For Women Leaders, Likability and Success Hardly Go Hand-in-Hand," *Harvard Business Review,* April 30, 2013, https://hbr.org/2013/04/for-women-leaders-likability-a.

4. Leah D. Sheppard and Karl Aquino, "Much Ado About Nothing? Observers' Problematization of Women's Same-Sex Conflict at Work," *Academy of Management Perspectives* 27, no. 1 (December 29, 2012), https://amp.aom.org/content/27/1/52.abstract.

5. Ann Friedman, "Shine Theory: Why Powerful Women Make the Greatest Friends, *Cut,* May 31, 2013, www.thecut.com/2013/05/shine-theory-how-to-stop-female-competition.html.

6. Shankar Vedantam, "Evidence of Racial, Gender Biases Found In Faculty Mentoring, *Morning Edition,* April 22, 2014, www.npr.org/2014/04/22/305814367/evidence-of-racial-gender-biases-found-in-faculty-mentoring.

7. Vivian Hunt, Dennis Layton, and Sara Prince, "Why Diversity Matters," McKinsey & Company, January 2015, www.mckinsey.com/business-functions/organization/our-insights/why-diversity-matters.

8. Alex Williams, "Why Is It Hard to Make Friends Over 30?" *New York Times,* July 13, 2012, www.nytimes.com/2012/07/15/fashion/the-challenge-of-making-friends-as-an-adult.html.

9. Rebecca Harris, "The Loneliness Epidemic: We're More Connected Than Ever—but Are We Feeling More Alone?," *Independent,* March 30, 2015, www.independent.co.uk/life-style/health-and-families/features/the-loneliness-epidemic-more-connected-than-ever-but-feeling-more-alone-10143206.html.

10. Gail Matthews, "Goals Research Summary," Dominican University of California, www.dominican.edu/academics/lae/undergraduate-programs/psych/faculty/assets-gail-matthews/researchsummary2.pdf.

11. Gretchen Rubin, *Better Than Before* (New York: Broadway Books, 2015), 21–22.

12. Michael L. Lowe and Kelly L. Haws, "(Im)moral Support: The Social Outcomes of Parallel Self-Control Decisions," *Journal of Consumer Research* 41, no. 2 (2014): 489–505.

13. Leonardo Bursztyn, Thomas Fujiwara, and Amanda Pallais, "The Ambition-Marriage Trade-Off Too Many Single Women Face," *Harvard Business Review,* May 8, 2017, https://hbr.org/2017/05/the-ambition-marriage-trade-off-too-many-single-women-face.

14. Ray Fisman, "Men Still Aren't Comfortable with Ambitious Women," *Slate,* December 22, 2016, www.slate.com/articles/news_and_politics/the_dismal_science/2016/12/men_still_aren_t_comfortable_with_ambitious_women.html.

15. Lora E. Park, Ariana F. Young, and Paul W. Eastwick, "(Psychological) Distance Makes the Heart Grow Fonder: Effects of Psychological Distance and Relative Intelligence on Men's Attraction to Women," *Personality and Social Psychology Bulletin* 41, no. 11 (August 24, 2015): 1459–1473, https://journals.sagepub.com/doi/abs/10.1177/0146167215599749.

16. Julianne Holt-Lunstad, Wendy Birmingham, and Brandon Q. Jones, "Is There Something Unique About Marriage? The Relative Impact of Marital Status, Relationship Quality, and Network Social Support on Ambulatory Blood Pressure and Mental Health," *Annals of Behavioral Medicine* 35, no. 2 (April 1, 2008): 239–244, https://academic.oup.com/abm/article-abstract/35/2/239/4569261.

Conclusion: You Have What You Need

1. Warren Buffett, "Warren Buffett Is Bullish . . . on Women," *Fortune,* May 2, 2013, http://fortune.com/2013/05/02/warren-buffett-is-bullish-on-women.

2. "Michelle Obama & Tracee Ellis Ross in Conversation at the 2018 United State of Women Summit," Facebook, May 6, 2018, www.facebook.com/TheUnitedStateofWomen/videos/michelle-obama-tracee-ellis-ross-in-conversation-at-the-2018-united-state-of-wom/1218311491636715.

Emilie Aries is an internationally recognized speaker and the founder and CEO of Bossed Up, an innovative personal and professional training organization that helps women craft sustainable careers.

Emilie hosts the biweekly *Bossed Up* podcast, where she interviews expert guests and helps listeners navigate all kinds of career conundrums. She previously served as the cohost of *Stuff Mom Never Told You*, the fiercely feminist podcast by HowStuffWorks, and served as a regular contributor at *Forbes, Huffington Post,* and Levo League.

Emilie is a political organizer turned award-winning women's leadership expert. She has helped hundreds navigate career transitions, prevent burnout, and achieve sustainable success.

Previously, Emilie served on national political campaigns as a digital strategist and grassroots organizer, where she trained and managed hundreds of organizers, helped campaigns leverage online communication technology, and smashed stereotypes about women in tech.

She earned her BA in political science from Brown University and completed a fellowship on organizing at the Harvard Kennedy School of Government. Emilie is based in Denver, Colorado, and combines her political instincts and personal experience with burnout to help women step into their power and be the boss of their lives.

PublicAffairs is a publishing house founded in 1997. It is a tribute to the standards, values, and flair of three persons who have served as mentors to countless reporters, writers, editors, and book people of all kinds, including me.

I. F. STONE, proprietor of *I. F. Stone's Weekly*, combined a commitment to the First Amendment with entrepreneurial zeal and reporting skill and became one of the great independent journalists in American history. At the age of eighty, Izzy published *The Trial of Socrates*, which was a national bestseller. He wrote the book after he taught himself ancient Greek.

BENJAMIN C. BRADLEE was for nearly thirty years the charismatic editorial leader of *The Washington Post*. It was Ben who gave the *Post* the range and courage to pursue such historic issues as Watergate. He supported his reporters with a tenacity that made them fearless and it is no accident that so many became authors of influential, best-selling books.

ROBERT L. BERNSTEIN, the chief executive of Random House for more than a quarter century, guided one of the nation's premier publishing houses. Bob was personally responsible for many books of political dissent and argument that challenged tyranny around the globe. He is also the founder and longtime chair of Human Rights Watch, one of the most respected human rights organizations in the world.

·   ·   ·

For fifty years, the banner of Public Affairs Press was carried by its owner Morris B. Schnapper, who published Gandhi, Nasser, Toynbee, Truman, and about 1,500 other authors. In 1983, Schnapper was described by *The Washington Post* as "a redoubtable gadfly." His legacy will endure in the books to come.

Peter Osnos, *Founder*